Charles M. Taintor

Extracts from the Records of Colchester

With some Transcripts from the Recording of Michaell Taintor

Charles M. Taintor

Extracts from the Records of Colchester
With some Transcripts from the Recording of Michaell Taintor

ISBN/EAN: 9783337186135

Printed in Europe, USA, Canada, Australia, Japan

Cover: Foto ©ninafisch / pixelio.de

More available books at **www.hansebooks.com**

EXTRACTS

FROM THE

RECORDS OF COLCHESTER,

WITH SOME TRANSCRIPTS

FROM THE RECORDING OF

MICHAELL TAINTOR,

OF "BRAINFORD," CONN.

Transcribed by
CHARLES M. TAINTOR.

HARTFORD:
PRESS OF CASE, LOCKWOOD AND COMPANY.
1864.

PREFACE.

THE beginning of the settlement of a Township is an important and interesting epoch in the history of a country : and its gradual progress is marked by events, a record of which is well worthy of being preserved in an available form, for all those who would pause for a moment, in this life's hurried journey, and reflect upon those who have gone before them, and occupied their places, and assumed the responsibilities that are now incumbent on themselves, in the highly favored place of their earthly abode : what their characters were, the influence they acquired and exercised over the minds of their contemporaries; the amount of knowledge they possessed ; and the degree of intelligence that guided and characterized them in all their pursuits and relations in life ; what the motives were by which they were actuated in forming a new settlement and the objects in the far distant future that determined their courses and inspired their hopes: the many trials they experienced, the dangers they cheerfully braved, the obstacles that presented themselves in various forms, the opposition they had to encounter, the hardships and privations they nobly endured ; the energy, perseverance and courage with which they at length overcame all untoward circumstances ; and the full measure of success that ultimately crowned their unwearied efforts. The voluntary association together of a body of men of the highest respectability, and of the first families from different parts of the country, in the planting of a Township, is a guaranty that something of great public benefit, something durable and far-reaching, something of high National importance and permanent utility is contemplated and viewed through the medium of long intervening time by the self-sacrificing and energetic men who thus forego the comforts and refinements of life, which have hitherto gladdened their pathway, for the noble and exalted purposes which inspired them. There is something extremely narrow-minded, unnatural and ungrateful in us of the present generation, who feel no interest in the shining lives and noble acts of our ancestors, through whose agency all of our high and invaluable rights and privileges were compassed and established ; who were instrumental in laying broad and deep and firm the foundations of our long-cherished institutions, and the whole enviable fabric, religious, social and educational which pervades and distinguishes New-England from other countries; and under her benign influence many others of the United States, through her sons and daughters who have settled in them. New-England is to the rest of America what Greece was to the surrounding nations of antiquity, the seat of science and the arts, learning, refinement, general intelligence and piety; and shall the names, lives and memories of her illustrious and noble founders, whose descendants many of us are, be lost, unrecorded and forgotten, and ignominiously suffered to mingle in the waters of oblivion? They were truly deserving of much at the hands of their descendants, for their lives were of as much importance as the lives of kings and the titled ones of the earth; their history would be as absorbing, and marked with events of as much consequence; and the history of the townships with which their history is identified is as interesting as the history of kingdoms. How little do we consider how largely we are indebted to our worthy progenitors for the inheritance of these beautiful towns and cities, and the whole surrounding country, adorned and beautified as it is, and rendered so attractive by the marks of cultivation, with our school-houses, meeting-houses and high seminaries of learning, wise, humane and equal laws, and the order, industry, general intelligence and virtue which characterizes the whole population, compared with that of many other parts of the world. All of these inestimable privileges, rich blessings, that so highly exalt us as a people, are the results of the wisdom, courage, perseverance and virtue of our fathers, who, in the dawn of learning and civilization in the New World, were the chosen agents for the establishment and dissemination of those elements.

To come nearer to the Township to which the following pages chiefly relate, one hundred and sixty-six years ago, Colchester was a primeval wilderness, with nothing to disturb its profound solitude but the Red man in quest of his game and fish, of which, there is no doubt, the forests, streams and ponds afforded a liberal supply for his simple necessities; and the whole adjacent country, from Massachusetts on the north to New London and Lyme on the south; and from Middletown, Glastenbury, Hartford, Windsor and Enfield on the west, to Norwich and Windham, was then one vast hunting-ground, over which roamed the savages in procuring their means of subsistence, and in traversing from one remote point of their lands to another, with an occasional village of wigwams, as the traces of them long subsequently afforded evidence. Here, at that period, the Indian held undisputed sway; but an era in their history and that of the white man was about to dawn. When our ancestors erected their habitations and commenced their permanent abode here, *then* was Colchester, in its unrivaled attractions, in its peerless beauty, and surpassing loveliness; with her far-famed and richly

endowed seminary, her elegant meeting-houses and private resi-
dences, her extensive manufactories and elevated society and refinement, in embryo—then was planted the germ that has since grown
up and expanded into what we behold of Colchester at this day. All
will feel constrained to acquiesce in the opinion that our forefathers
possessed no small degree of good sense, penetration and foresight
in selecting so naturally charming a site for their future abode: so
highly susceptible of being beautified and adorned.

The Connecticut State Records at the Office of the Secretary of
State furnish us with the date of the Grant and settlement of Colchester, and contain much in relation to the troubles that the planters
of Colchester experienced, and the difficulties they met with in
establishing the boundaries of the Township, and the opposition and
perplexity they encountered from Owaneco and Joshua, the Mohegan Chiefs, who were the sons of the great warrior, Uncas, and
from the Masons, Major Palmes and many others, who claimed large
tracts of land within the Grant, by virtue of titles and grants obtained from the heirs of the great Mohegan Sachem, Uncas.

" Att a Generall Court Holden at Hartford Octobr the 13th:
1698 : This Court upon the petition of Divers of the inhabitants in
the Countie of Hartford Grant Libertye for a plantation at or near
the place Called Jeremiahs farme upon the Rode to Newlondon.
and Captn Danll Wetherell Captn John Hamlin Mr Will Pitkin
Captn John Chester Mr Richard Christophers and Captn Samll
ffosdick they or the Majr part of them are by this Court appointed
to be a Comittee to lay out a town Ship there beginning at the
North bound of twentie mile River and So to Extend Southward to a
River Called deep River And to Extend Eastward from the bounds
of Haddum Seven miles"—

" Att a Generll assembly Holden att Hartford May 11th 1699—
Ordered and Enacted &c that the north bounds of the new Plantation Lately granted at or neer Jeremies farme upon the Roade to
Newlondon Shall be (as formerly at twentye mile River, and the
South bounds ioyne to the North bounds of Lyme, and the west
bounds to Joyn to the East bounds of Middltown and the East
bounds of Haddum and the East and North East bounds to Rune
to the bounds of Lebanon and Norwich"—

" A Generall Assembly Holden at Hartford Octor 13,, 1699—
Michael Taintor Saml Northam and Nath,l Foot appearing in this
Assembly in the behalfe of the New plantation called Colchester and
complaining that they are obstructed in the improvement and settlement of said plantation by reason of severall persons that claim considerable tracts of land within the grant of said Township, and par-
ticularly severall of the inhabitants of Saybrook, This Court do
therefore order that all persons claiming any lands there shall appear at the Generall Court in May next and make their claims appear, that so the Grantees may not be further obstructed in their
settlement of said plantation and that the name of that plantation

1*

shall be called Colchester and belong to the County of New London, and further that this act be transmitted to the severall towns where any persons claiming land, there doe reside that so they may have reasonable notice thereof."

"Att a Generall Assembly Holden att Hartford Octobr the 10th: 1700 Whereas the Inhabitants of Colchester and those designed to goe and Settle there, meet, with much discouragement in their Planting and Settling By Owaneco and the Moheags, that Claim Land within that township. This assembly being Sensible of the difficulties they meet with and being desirous to promote the Quiet and Comfortable Settlement of the Plantation Doe desire the Honble Governr with his Councill to treat with the Moheags and to agree with them to Quitt their Claim to the Lands within that township, upon as Reasonable termes as may be obtained and also to advise the people and to direct them in going forward in their Plantation worke, and the Worshipfull Captn Samuel Mason is desired to improve his Interest in the Moheags to Promote their Compliance with the Interest of the people of Colchester—The Charge to be defrayed by the Inhabitants of Colchester—"

Thus the whole Township of ancient Colchester, embracing the present Township, and portions of Salem (in olden time called Paugwonk) and Marlborough, was granted to the original planters, and by them subsequently shared with their associate planters. Then followed divisions of the Township at intervals of time amongst the proprietors, a certain portion of the territory being included in a division. A division was then subdivided into allotments or Rights, consisting of fifty, one hundred and two hundred pound rights for which the proprietors cast lots, the number in the Draught determining for each proprietor his claim to a corresponding number in the allotments. In this way half a century, or more, elapsed before the whole Township had been divided amongst the original planters and proprietors, and the heirs of those of them who had deceased.

The lands, of little value comparatively, at the beginning of the settlement, gradually increased in value as the population and demand for land increased: and those of the proprietors and their descendants and heirs, who retained their rights in the divisions of lands, became substantially wealthy and prosperous. Colchester was a highly popular settlement, and the early planters were a superior set of men, belonging, as they did, to many of the first families in New England: and it early attracted a brilliant array of names and genius from various parts of the country. Its location was desirable, being near Hartford, Middletown, Norwich and New London.

Micaiell Taintor, Esq., whose recording comprises the chief portion of these pages, was born in Brainford, Oct.,—A. D. 1652, being the second son of Capt. Michaell Taintor and his wife Elizabeth. We have no knowledge of his youthful history. We find him in

Windsor in A. D. 1679, where he married Mary, daughter of Thomas Loomis, and after her decease Mabel (Olmstead) Butler, widow of Mr. Daniel Butler of Hartford, in A. D. 1697. He was one of the leading men in Windsor, as appears by the records of that Town, holding some of the highest offices in that Township. He was, doubtless, one of the most active in procuring the Grant of Colchester, being in the prime of life when he removed to that place to settle. He was the first, and for a long series of years the only Justice of the Peace in Colchester; Town Clerk for the space of thirty years, member of Conn. General Assembly twenty-six sessions; Commissioner, Selectman, &c. It should be borne in mind that in those days honors and offices were conferred with reference to worth of character, only the best and most fit men being found in high stations. Then men honored an office, unlike the present day, when we find *mankind* seeking offices and honors through mercenary channels, to patch up characters obnoxious to scrutiny under the eternal standard of rectitude, the immutable law of Justice, and our Saviour's Golden Rule. He died Feb.,—A. D. 1731, in his 79th year.

His father, Michaell, was also a man of sterling worth and integrity of character, having acquired and exerted a high-toned influence over his contemporaries. He was the son of Charles Taintor who was in Wethersfield in A. D. 1643, afterward Deputy to Gen. Assembly, two years, from Fairfield, and who was lost at sea with Mr. Jeremiah Jagger in Oct., A. D. 1654. Michaell was Master of a Ketch, trading out of Brainford to Virginia previous to A. D. 1650, and for several years subsequent. He was Commissioner, Judge, Deputy to Gen. Assembly, Recorder, Select-man, &c. He died in —A. D. 1672–3.

Rev. John Bulkley was from Glastenbury, son of Rev. Gurshom and his wife, (who was a daughter of President Chauncey) and grandson of Rev. Peter Bulkley, from England. "Isaac Bigloo" was from Watertown Mass. "John Bigloo a son of Joshua Bigloo of Watertown, which John Bigloo now dwells in Hartford on the east." Thomas Carrier and his sons, Richard and Andrew, were from Andover, where Martha, wife of Thomas, was executed for a witch, in A. D. 1692. Thomas Carrier had belonged to the body guard of King Charles 1st of Great Britain, and was notorious for fleetness of foot, even after he was more than one hundred years old. It is said that he killed the king of England. If so, he must have been the executioner of King Charles the 1st, in A. D. 1648. He was a Welshman. It is said by his descendents that he was one hundred and thirteen years of age at the time of his decease in A. D. 1735. Daniel Clark, "Locksmith," was from Hartford—Samuel Dickinson from Hadley—Jonathan Dunham from Haddam—Foots were from Wethersfield—Samuel Gilbert from Hartford—Benjamin Graves from New London, doubtless, originally from Hatfield—Josiah Gillet and Josiah Gillet Jun., from Windsor. The wife of

Josiah Sen., was Joanna, daughter of Michaell Taintor of Brainford. She died in Colchester, in Jan., A. D. 1735, aged 83 years. John Hitchcock from Springfield—Evan Jones from Windsor?—Kelloggs from Hatfield—Loomises from Windsor — James and Israel Newton from "Kingstown in Naraganset"—"Samuel Niels" of Kingstown (1709)—Northams from Hatfield—Nathaniel Otis from Scituate—Josiah Phelps from Windsor—"Joseph Pumery" from Northampton?—William Shipman from Saybrook, went to Hebron about 1705, where he soon after died in consequence of a fall.—Skinners from Hartford?—Deac. ."Micaell" Taintor from Windsor—James Treadway, "Malster," from Watertown—Welleses from Hatfield—Joseph Wright from Glastenbury—Israel Wyatt from Hatfield.

In conclusion, the compiler would say that Colchester and its history present more than ordinary attractions to him, inasmuch as it was the home and the birth-place of many of his ancestors besides of those whose surname he bears. He traces his descent from " Quarter-Master Nathaniel Foot," who took an active part in promoting the settlement of Colchester; from Nathaniel Loomis, Sen., and from Nathaniel Loomis, Jr., (the schoolmaster)—from Samuel and Ebenezer Northam—from——Skinner—from Lieut. Noah Welles who died in A. D. 1713, and Lieut. Noah Wells who died in A. D. 1753, and Col. David Wells; and from Lieut. Israel Wyatt the son of John Wyatt of Haddam, and grandson of Edward Wyatt of Dorchester.

CHARLES MICAIELL TAINTOR.

Colchester, Conn., Feb. 13th, A. D. 1864.

THE RECORDING OF MICAIELL TAINTOR ESQ.

"JENEWARY the 28th 1715=16=then Jonathan kilburn of Colchester presented a mare and coult to Record as straise—the mare is of a Dark Brown Coulour Branded with Lebanon town Brand a half penne Cut on the vnder side of the of or Right eare—the Coult is a hors Coult of a Bay Couler a star in the forehead near foot white—taken Dammage fezant: & now aprised both at fowr pounds—By James Mun & Josiah Phelps—the mare & Coult Aboue mentioned is owned By Joshua Tilleson of hebron & Delivered to him by sd kilburn this 1 Day of March 1715-16

June 12th 1716 then taken vp By Ebenezer Spencer of Colchester A yong hors of about two or thre years old of a blackish Brown Couler Branded with :4: marked with a half pennee Cut on the under sid of the Right eare: of foot behind white—Taken vp in a sufering Condistion: & aprised this eighteenth Day of June abouesd: at twenty five shillings by William Worthington & Daniell Clark Junr

May 1716 Josiah Gate killed 18 Rattell snakes

at the meeting mentioned on the other side viz. Decembr 28: 1713 Samull Northam thomas Day & ebenezer Colman ware chosen a Comittie of the school for the year insueing.

Decemb: 31: 1712: at a legall town meeting held in Colchester—Capt Gilbert Left Wiat & Mr Dainell Clark ware Chosen Selectmen: Decembr 28: 1713: Micaiell Taintor was

2

Chosen towne Clerk for the year insueing: at a legall town meeting held in Colchester the date aforesaid: at the same meeting selectmen ware chosen Namely mr Daniell Clark senr: mr Joseph Wright & Micaiell Taintor—Constables Chosen ware Nathaniell Kellogg & ebenezer Skiner—sworn—Colecterors to Colect the minestors Rate & town rate John Bigloo Noah wells & Jonathan kellogg—fence vewers Chosen ware John hitchcock & william Chamberlin—Surueyers Chosen ware: John Johnson sworn—Andrew Carrier sworn—Ephream foot sworn—Ephream Wells sworn—John homes & Samll Spencer—Listers chosen ware thomas Day Richard Skiner & John hubberd—all sworn—enspectors Chosen ware ebenezer Colman & Daniell Clark Juner—both sworn—Grand Jury men Chosen ware John addams sener Nathanll Lomis—both sworn—" further at the meeting aforesaid the town granted a Rate of 3d pence on the pownd of the ratebl estate of the towne—at the meeting aforesaid the towne granted to the Reuerant Mr Bulkly for his salery the year past sixty and five pownds—at the same meeting a Comitie was Chosen to setell the Line with hebron men betwixt hebron and Colchester—namely ebenezer Skiner Left Wiat ensine Skiner ebenezer Colman Nathanll foot—

February the 24th: 1713—14:

taken vp as strays by Josiah Gillet of Colchester a mare & Coult: the mare is Counted about seauen or eight years old of a sorrell Couler a white face & a streak of white downe the houf on the left foot—Branded on the left shoulder with MM: the Could is one year and vantage old of a sorrell Couler a White face 2 hind feet white no mark nor brand—

apprised at four pownds ten shillings

By Daniell & Nathaniell Clark

July 13th 1716—Sold a black stone hors of thre years old brought in by thomas perrin of Lebanon: as forfit by law: & Condemned By us the subscribers selectmen: as not being so high as the law Requiers: sold to ensign Nathanll lomis for thre pownds six shillings: Micaiell Taintor—Samull Lomies

Micaiell Taintor Junr Creded for seruing thre writs: (viz.) on bakon gates & homes—00–06 00 one on sergt Rowle: 6d: for half my Jorney & exspences to Wethersfield to fetch nailes—00 04 00 by two shillings Guien to bye Boards—00 02 00

1713 Mr Thomas Alleson Credet to the town for nailes for the meeting hows Doars—00 03 06

December ye 8th 1729 Micaiell Taintor was chosen Town clerk Ensign Foot Ensign Wells & Israel Newton ware Chosen Selectmen—Constables Chosen Ware Joseph Chamberlin & he to gather the Contry Rate & Isaac Jones—Way Wardens Chosen Ware John hitchcock Samuell Lomis John biglow Joseph pratt Junr pelatiah bliss andrew Carier—grand jurymen Chosen ware Jonathan Gillett & noah pumery—Listers Chosen ware mr Nathanll Otis John holms noah Clark timothy Carrier and John skiner Junr—fence viewers Chosen ware thomas adams & nathaniell kellogg Junr—tithing men Chosen Samuell fuller Josiah strong—a town Rate granted of a half penne Rate—yt is to say a half pene on ye pownd to be Raised as the law directs—Colecters to gather sd rate ware Ebenezer kellogg & Daniell Worthington,

at a town meeting held in Colchester Aprell 28th: 1730 ensign Nathaniell foot was Chosen moderator of sd meeting—at the meeting it was voated that swine shold be Confined from going at larg in the Comons as the law directs and prouids in yt behalf for this present yeare—further voated yt shepe may go in the Comons without a keeper for this present year—the meeting is adjorned untill the monday before the election (viz ye eleauenth Day of May next at twelue of the Clock—the town met acording to adjornmt—& voated & granted to ye Reuerend mr John Bulkley that thre acers of land lying at the rear of his home lot (formerly granted for a term of years: but now the town grant it to him for euer on Condistion that he giue up so much as that is of his other land) to be & Remain to be Comons for euer—further at ye same meeting the town voated to Remit the towns part of the fine of ebenezer harthaway Samuell Day John Dale John Adams ye 3d & Daniell Adams—at the same meeting it was voated yt wharas at ye meeting abuesd (abovesaid–c. m. t.) viz Aprell 28th 1730 Ensin Nathanll foot John Bulkley Junr & William Roberds ware Chosen a Comitie with power to treat with a Comitie from labanon Respecting such Controuersis as are now Depending in ye law or other wise betwen the proprieters of this town & the proprieters of labanon & finally to determine the same & to agre upon a line betwen us & them & wharas ye sd Comitie haue on the eighth Day of this Instant may treated & Com to an agrement with a Comitie from labanon & now make Report thareof to this meeting—it was voated yt ye sd agrement be exsepted & yt in all ye parts thareof it be Complyed with & yt it be entered on ye town Records—

A list of the freemen of ye town of Colchester—Micaiell Taintor Micaiell Taintor Junr James Newton Samll Northam Thom Day Richd Carrier Ebenezr Skiner Danll Clark Danll Clark Junr Lef Isreall Wyat Decon Lomis Wm Roberds Nathll Lomis Jos Wright Josiah Gellet Josiah Gillet Junr Ebenezer Dibell Capt Gilbert Jno Adams Jno adams Junr Decon Skiner Richd Skiner Nathanll Skiner Benjamin Skiner Jos Prat Nathll Kellogg Ephrem Foot Jos pumery Thom Brown Noah Wells Jos Chamberlin Josiah Foot James mun ensign Jno Skiner Ebenezer kellogg James Brown Andrew Carrier Richard Church Mr Bulkley Jno Day Jonathan Gillet Jonathan Kellogg Nathll Foot Ebenr Coleman Charles Williams Clement Cithophell John Chapman Senr Ephream Wells Josiah Phelps John holms William Roberds Josiah Gates Joseph foot John Johnson—

At a Legall town meeting held in Colchester Nouembr the

9th : 1714: the towne voated that whearas we formerly granted
our lands to perticqler persons by a towne voat we now Do
voat that for the future The granting of the undeuided lands
in Colchester shall be wholy and solely in the power of the
proprioters of Colchester—at the same meeting the town made
Choice of Mr James Newton Samuel Northam Samll Lomis
Joseph Wright & Ebenezer Coleman to be a Committie to
prosecute in the law & eject any & euery person that doe or
shall trespass or make enterance uppon any of the Deuided or
undeuided Lands within the township of said Colchester

Decembr ye 27 1714 was a towne meeting & Micaiell Taintor Sen was Chosen town Clerk for the year Insueing—Selectmen Chosen ware Mr Daniell Clark Senr Mr James Newton
& ensign Jno Skiner—Constables chosen and sworn ware
Thomas Day & nathaniell Kellogg—Colectorors Chosen to
gather the minesters Rate & town rate ware Jonathan Northam James Newton Junr and Richard Church—granted to
the Reuerant Mr Bulkley for his salery the year now almost
past the sum of seauenty & thre pownds Curant Mony—ondly
eight pownds of it is to find himself firewood for the year Insueing—Listers chosen ware Benjamin adams Nathaniel Gilbert Samuell Lomis Junr—Inspecters Chosen & sworn ware
John Bigloo & Noah Weles—Surueyers Chosen & sworn
ware Capt Gilbert John biglo Isreall Newton William Roberds Junr Jonathan Kellog & Daniell Clark Junr—Grand
Juremen Chosen and sworn ware Left Isreall Wyat Nathanill
foot—fenc vewers Chosen & sworn ware Josiah Gillet Junr
& Isaac Dauice Ephream foot & Josiah phelps—further the
towne voated & Chose a Comitie to settell the Bounds Betwixt
east haddam & Colchester the Comitie Chosen ware ensign
John Skiner Mr James Newton & Mr Daniell Clark senr—
and also the same Comitie to settell & run the Bounds Betwixt Midell Towne & Colchester—at the sam meeting aforesaid the towne voated & Granted to Nathaniell Lomis six

2

pownds more then that forty & one pownds which the Comitie
Couenanted with him for the makeing the seats of the meeting howse & other work mentioned in the sd Couenant—at
the same meeting the towne granted a rate of two penc on
the pownd to defray the town charges to be raised & Leuied
by the list giuen unto the generall Court in October last past—
at the same meeting Joseph Chamberlin John Skiner and Nathaniell Kellogg ware Chosen a Comitie for the schole for the
year Insueing—at the same meeting leften.t Wiatt Capt Gilbert Mr James Newton Joseph Pumery & Joseph Chamberlin ware chosen seators to seate persons in the meeting hows—

Jeneway the 4th 1714–15 was a legall town meeting &
whearas theare was a towne meeting dec 27–1714 & there
was seators Chosen to seats the Meeting howse: : but no ruels
(rules c. m. t.) giuen them as to do the work neigehther haue
the towne Dignefied the seats of the sd howse—therefore the
towne haue now Dignefied the first pue next the pulpit to be
the first in dignety the next behind it to be the 2d in dignety
& the foremost of the long seats to be the third in Dignety :
the 4th In dignetie is the second long seat & the third pue
these two to be equall in estemation : the third seat to be the
next In Dignety—the fourth seat to be next In dignety : the
next seat in Dignety is the fourth pue : the next in dignety is
the fifth long seate—the next thing is the Rules in seating &
the Rules are now agreed & voated as foloweth—first the 12d :
& 3d Rate for buelding the meeting hows to be Considered
in Conjuntion with the present List of estates—further in the
next place age with other quallefiecations to be considered—
at the same meeting abouesd Ephream wels & John Bigloo :
further it was voated that the seators shall also Consider the
last years List with ye other abouementioned—at the same
meeting abouesaid the persons : Chosen for the seating persons
in the meeting howse are the same persons chosen formerly
(viz) in Decembr 27th : 1714 are Also now againe Chosen to

yt work: who are to do it acording to the Dignifieing the
Seats & the Ruels of seating abouementioned—at the meeting
aforesaid the towne voated to guie for the Incoragement of persons to kill wolus. to guie twenty phillings a head .for wolues
killed in the Bounds of the towne: the heads Bought as the
law directs—whearas the towne at the meeting mentioned on
the opposite side did Dignefi the seats in the meeting hows:
& the Comitie haue presented to the town a draught with
alteration in the sd Dignefieing the seats the town now being
met together: Jenewary ye 10th: 1714-15 Did exsept of the
alteration mad By said Comittie which is as followeth: the pue
next ye pulpitt to be the first—2d in dignety is the 2d pue &
the fore seat to be equall In Dignetie. 3d in Dignety is the
second seat—4th: : is the third seat equall with ye third Pue
—5. is the fowrth seat equall with the fowrth Pue—next the
fifth seat: next: 6th–7th–8th—

Colchester June 28 1715 at A meeting of the towne & pro-
priotors of Colchester the sd towne & proprioters chose mr
Jams Newton Ensign John Skiner & ebenezr Colman A
Comittie to Joyne with a Commitie of east haddam to make
exshang of Land—for the beter Conuenienc of both places—
to make Alteration of the bounds Lately Run By the County
Surueyer as thay shall se Cause & the sd town & proprioters
do agree to abide by such alterations as shall be agreed upon
By the sd Comities of Both parties—at the meeting aforesaid
the town voated to giue the select men the Power to appoynt
the place whare all persons shall Cut bushes that the Law Requiers to work in that seruice

at A Legall town meeting held in Colchester the 26th Day
of Decembr 1715 the town granted a Rate of two penc on the
povnd to be raised on all the poles & Ratable estate acording
to the present List of this present year: to be paid in or as
mony: to Defray the town charges—at the said meeting
Micaiell Taintor was chosen Town Clerk—the select men

Chosen ware Left John Skiner Micaiell Taintor senr & Decon
Lomis—Constables Chosen were Daniell Clark Junr & Josiah
Gillett Jun—Colecterers Chosen to gather the Minesters &
town Rate were Jonathan Gillett and thomas Lomis : & that
Each of them shall gather & be Responcable for the Rats in
that part of the town where they Dwell : the Dcuision Betwene them to Be acording to the Deuiding Line betwixt the
two train Bands of the towne—Surueyers or way wardens
Chosen ware Jonathan Kilbun Josia foot Thom Jones John
Day Jno hitchcock Ebenezer Coleman—Listers Chosen &
sworn ware Nathaniell Lomis Junr Thomas Day Junr & Joseph Pepoon—fenc vewers chosen were Ephraim foot & Clement kithophell—grand-Jurymen Chosen & sworn ware Sergt
Joseph Prat sergt Nathaniell kellogg—at the Same Meeting
the town granted to sergt Nathaniell kellogg thirty shillings pr
year for sweeping & looking after the meeting howse as it
ought to Bee—at the aforesd meeting the town Granted the
Reuer-t Mr Bulkley for his salery the year Past eighty pownds
mony or prouision as mony—at the same Meeting the town
Chose the Select men Now Chosen to Be a Comitie for the
School for The year Ensueing—

at a town meeting June 12th 1716 it was voated to finish the
schole hows whare the foundation of the said hows now stands—
We the select men Comittie for the schooll as abouesaid haue
agreed with Nathaniell Lomis Juner to keepe school twelue
month & to giue him twenty and fiue pownds ten shillings—
25–10–0 & he began to keep schooll ye 17th Day of Jeneway :
1716—the minesters Rate : & town Rate Deliuered to the
forementioned Colecterors to gather & pay acording to order.

Jeneway the 8th : 1716 : 17=was a towne meeting &
Micaiell Taintor senr was Chosen town Clerk for the year
ensuing=at the same meeting : Benjamin Lewes John Clother
Isaac Biglow John hitchcock Thomas Jones Benjamin Graues
John Jonson ware exsepted and admitted Inhabetanc on Con-

dision that thay now declareing that thay do not nether will
not hearafter Claime any Right to the vndeuided Lands in
Colchester neighther to the stated Commons: by this admition
—which they haue now declared & Consented to—Select men
Chosen ware capt Newton .Jos: Chamberlin & Left Skiner:
Constabels Chosen and sworn ware Daniell Clark Junr & Josiah Gillet Junr—Colecterors to Gather the minesters & town
Rate ware Andrew Carrier & Benjamin Graues—.Listers
chosen and sworn ware : John hitchcock Isaac Rowlee—Samell kellogg not sworn—Grand Jury chosen & sworn ware ensign: Weles & Ebenezer skiner—fenc vewers chosen ware
Jonathan kilburn & John Adams Jur—Way wardens Chosen
& sworn all but: ware James Roberds Jno Clother william
Chamberlin not sworn—William harris Thomas Jones Ebenezer Dibell John Chapman senr & Ensin Lomis—At the meeting aforesaid : Daniell Clark Juner was chosen & sworn sealer
of waits & Measurs — At the meeting Aforesaid the town
Granted to the Reuerand Mr bulkley for his sallery for the
year past the sum of eighty pownds in mony or in prouision
pay as mony—at the meeting Aforesaid the town voated to
Raise a Rate of one penne on the pownd to pay the town
Debts—further at the same meeting it was voated to maintain
a school the whole year: and that It be kept at thre seuerall
places (viz) in the town plat & at the hill as it is Called (&
amongst the southerly farmers) each Inhabetant in euery part
to Joyne to which part or place as he shall chouse : and each
seuerall place whare the school is kept shall haue the school
kept there so long as their proportion of estates is in the Comon
List—& each place To prouid a sutabell place or hows to keep
school in—& If eighther place Neglect to Comply with these
Artecles then the Comittie hearafter named shall haue full
power to order the afair of the school as thay in thair prudence
shall se Cause & the present select men are now Chosen a
Comitie for the school this year.

2*

At a Legall town meeting held in Colchester Decembr 30th: 1717 Micaiell Taintor was Chosen town Clerk—at the same meeting Mr Joseph Chamberlin Sergt Ebenezer Skiner & sergt Nathaniell foot ware chosen select men—Constables Chosen & sworn ware Sergt Joseph Pratt & ephraim foot Joseph Pratt to gather the Country Rate—Thomas Addams & ebenezer Northam Ware Chosen Colecterours to Gather the Town & Minesters Rate—Listers Chosen ware Isreall Newton James Roberds & Samuell Brown—sworn—Grand jure men Chosen ware John Addams Junr & James Newton Junr—sworn—fence vewers Chosen ware Jonathan Northam & John hitchcock— sworn Way wardens Chosen ware ensign Nathaniel Lomis Richard Church sworn Thomas Jones John waters William Chamberlin Josiah Gates Richard Carier & Josiah foot—sworn —Clement kithophell Chosen to Digg Graues—further at the same meting the town Granted To the Reu.rt Mr Bulkley tor his salery for The year Past eighty Pounds in mony or prouision Pay as mony—further voated to Giue Benjamin Chamberlin ten shillings for beating the Drum ye year Past—further voated that sergt Prat shall haue twenty shillings for sweeping and taking Care of the meeting hows the year ensueing—At the meeting Aforesaid it was voated And agreed that thare should Be Galeries Buelt: in the meeting hows with all Conuenient Speed—& Mr Charels Williams mr Samuell Northam & Sergt Nathaniell kellogg ware Chosen a Comitie to Carie on the work of buelding & finishing the said Galleries—further the town Granted a Rate of three half Pennys on the Pound to Defray town Charges—and finally it was voated that the surueyors of high waies shall haue Power to Call forth labourers to make a Bridg ouer the North meadow.

Decembr ye 22: 1718 was a Legall town meeting held in Colchester: Micaiell Taintor Senr was chosen Town Clerk for the year ensueing—Selectmen * * * William Worthington Joseph Chamberlin & John Skiner—Constables * * * Sergt

Joseph pratt & Ephreaim foot—Sergt Joseph prat to gather the
Country Rate—Colecterers * * John Day & thom Jones—
Listers Isaac Jones & John Northam—Grand Jurimen Decon
Lomis & ebenezer kellogg—Way wardens John Johnson John
biglow Noah Weles Robart Ransom Samuell Lomis Jvnr Samuel brown & lef holmes—farther at ye same meeting James
Newton Jvnr was chosen brander for the town of Colchester—
fenc vewers Chosen ware Benjamin adams & samuel kellogg—
at the same meeting Left-nt holms Leftent harris Daniell Jones
thomas Carier Samuell Knight Joseph Dalee : Daniell galutiah
ware voated Inhabetance : on that Condistion that Benjamin
Lewes & others ware exsepted :

at a town meeting held in Colchester Jenewary ye 8th :
1716—17 : further voted that the select men be the school
Comittie for ye year Insuing—At the meeting mentioned on
the other side the town voated and granted to the Reuerend
mr John Bulkley for his sallery for the yeare now almost past
eighty pownds in mony or prouision pay as mony—further
voated to giue and grant to the Reuerand Mr bulkley for his
sallery for the yeare ensueing eighty pownds in mony or prouision pay as mony prouided he Continue in the work of the
minestry Amongst us the yeare ensuing abouesaid—further at
the same meeting the town voated that euery person to whome
the towne is Indebted that if thay do not bring in thair acoumlt
to ye select men at the hows of Joseph Chamberlins this Day
fortnight : thay shall not be paid the yeare now ensueing—further the town granted to Sergnt pratt twenty shillings : to take
ye care of the meeting hows & sweep it sutabley : for the year
ensuing—further at the same meeting the town voated to oblige
euery person in the town of sixteen years of age and upwards
to kill one Duson of blackbirds or wood peckers or gay burds :
& bring thair heads to the select men : & what are killed in the
months of march aprell or may : six shall be Counted as a
duson : : & if any person kills more then his Duson he shall
be alowed one penne pr head—& he that doth not kill his dusen

as abouesd shall pay to the town Rate one shilling—this order to Continue for the year next ensuing—further voated that no ratell snaks shall be paid for exsept thay Can satisfie the select men that thay were killed in the months of aprell or may.

Colchester Janewary the 26th : 1718=19 was a Legall town meeting : & it was voated that Mr Liyn (?) : chool master shall be paid for keeping school for the time past : that which is Due : which is about six pounds—the one half out of the town tresury & the other half to be payd by the Scollers that went to the Said School—further at the same meeting the town voated to keep a school this whoole year—& that it shall be kept remoued unto thre seuerall parts of the town at the Discrestion of the select men—further at the meeting aforesaid it was further voated : that All the children from five years oald to the age of ten years that liue within one mile and half from the place whare the school is kept, shall pay to the sd school as the law Directs : whether thay go to said School or nott—& those that are aboue ten years of age shall pay ondly for the time as thay do go—further it was voated that the Colecterours shall be acountable to the town : their proportion in gathering the min_ esters & town Rate : in perticqler that is to say John Day to gather or Colect the Rates all that are within the limits of the bounds of Capt wrights train band : & thomas Jones : to gather all within the bounds of Captain Newtons train band : which the sd Colecterours define—further the town abated benjamin graues Jonathan Cutlers & benjamin foxes minesters & town Rats : which he was to gather.

at a legall town meeting held in Colchester Nouember ye 3d 1719=we being Informed that at a town meeting held at hebron the sd town voated to Choose a Comittie of thre men of thair town as a Comitie to settell a deuiding line betwixt ye sd town of hebron & the town of Colchester prouided said Colchester will also choose a Comitie of thre men of our town to Joyne with the Comitie of said hebron to settell ye line and

to End that Controuersi—it was now voated by the town to
Complie with the motion of ye town of hebron—& now to
proseed to Choos a Comittie to Joyne with a Comitie that the
town of hebron shall Choos to Consider & Isue yt matter of
the line as abouesaid & Leftent John Skiner : Sert Nathaniell
foot & Sergt Ebenezer Skiner ware chosen a Comitie to Joyn
with a Comitie of the town of hebron in setling the line abouesaid—& further it was voated to stant to and abide by the line
that may be agreed upon by the Said Comitie.

December 16th : 1719 : a Legall town meeting held in Colchester for the choice of town offecers (as followeth) Micaiell
Taintor was chosen town clerk—Select men, Capt Newton Lef
Skiner & Cap wright—Constables Sergt Joseph pratt & Noah
Wells—sergt prat to gather the Contry Rate & make up
acounts with the tresurer—grandjurimen Joseph pumery &
william worthington — Colecterers ebenezer dible & Isreall
Newton—ebenezer dible to Colect the Rats of the Persons be-
longing to Cap Wrights Company acording to the bounds in
the diuision of the train bands : betwixt Capt Newtons Com-
pany & said Capt Wrights Company: & Isreall Newton to
gather the Rats of ye Persons belonging to Capt Newtons
Company acording to the bounds abouesd=Way Wardens—
Nathaniell foot Ensin Lomis Samuel knight Daniell Jones John
Day John Wells ebenezer spencer—Listers—James Tredway
& Joseph prat Junr—fenc vewers John Jonson & Cornelis
Roberds—sealer of measurs Micaiell Taintor was chosen—
sealer of waits Daniell Clark Juner was chosen—at the meeting mentioned on the other side Decon Lomis was Chosen
Leather Sealer—further the town voated & chose a Comitie to
treat with the reuerant Mr bulkley Relating to his standing salery for his work in the minestry amongst us & make Return to
the town—the Comitie Chosen ware the present select men &
Samuell Northam : Decon Lomis & Micaiell Taintor further
it was voated that whereas at a town meeting held in Colchester

Nouember ye 3d 1719 the town Chose a Comitie to Joyn with a Comitie of the town of hebron in setling a Line to be the bounds betwixt the town of Colchester & the town of hebron and to stand to the bounds that may be fixed by the said Comittis it is now further voated that in Case the said Comities Canot agre: in fixing the bounds: then it shall be in the power of our Comitie : to Joyn with the Comittie of hebron in chousing thre men such as thay agree uppon to determin that Controuersie: & to stand to & abide by the line & bounds which said thre men shall fix for the Deuiding line betwixt the towns abouesaid—further it was voated to Raise a Rate of one penne on the pound on the Ratabell estate in the town to defray the town Charges.

Decembr 27th: 1720 was a legall town meeting in Colchester wherein Micaiell Taintor was chosen town Clerk for the year ensueing—select men—Capt Newton Ensign Wells & left Wyat—Constables sergt pratt & Noah wells—Surueyors—John Jonson Nathanill Cohoon John Northam Nathaniell Gilbert Ebenezer kellogg Sergt Isaac Jones John Chapman Junr Left John holms—fenc vewers thomas addams & Samuell kellogg—Listers, Capt Wright & sergt Nathanill Foot—Colecterors Samuell Knight & William Williams & to Deuide in gathering the Rates acording to the voat last year : Grand Jurymen Micaiell Taintor Junr & Clement kithophell—howards—Ephream foott & John Jonson—at the meeting aforesaid voated to grant Mr Bulkley Eighty pounds—at the meeting aforesaid the town voated that swine should go at larg in the Comons acording to the former law—at the meeting mentioned on the other side Sergt pratt was chosen & appoynted to take the Care of the meeting hows to keep the glass windows in repaire & to do what elce is of nesesety : & to make sutabell steps at the dores —& to be payd out of the town tresury. : furder at the meeting aforesd it was voated that the town meeting to chous town offecers for the futuer shall be on the second munday of decembr anually & the select men are to set up a notefication thereof ten days before yt time on the end of the scool house—at the meeting aforesaid sergt ebenr Dible Sargt Nathaniell foot & John biglow ware chosen to Inspect into the encrochments made by persons: by fencing & takeing into their Improuement the town high-ways: & also takeing into thayr Improuement further & more then was layd out to them: in their other Deuisions of land: & said Comittie shall giue such persons Reasonable notice to thro up or Remoue thayr fence—that so the town in generall may be benefited there by—& if any person or persons shall neglect to lay to the Comons: such land: so Incroached: eighther in the town street or in: deuisions of land thay are hearby Impowered to prosecute: any such person in the law for thayr so doing.

March ye 20th: 1721: was a Legall town meting held in Colchester—the town voated to Raise a Rate of one penne on the pound, acording to the present List: to be disposed of to pay the nesesary charges arising this present year: (viz: the school and to the finishing the galleries & other charges—at the same meeting the town voated that the Comitie Aboue mentioned shall haue further power: then what is aboue mentioned [Viz] thair power shall extend to the town Comons stated By the proprioters at thair meeting Sept ye 30th 1715: acording to the bounds then prescribed & to extend no further—further the town Chose sergt kellogg sergt pratt & Daniell Clark a Comitie to Carie on the finishing of the galleries of the meeting hows.

Decembr ye 11th: 1721 at a Legall town meeting held in Colchester for the Choice of town officers—Micaiell Taintor was chosen town Clerk—Select men Capt Newton ensign wells & Left wyat—Constables Noah Weels & ensign foot Grandjurie men Samull Lomis Junr & William Roberds Junr—Surueyers of higwaise Nathaniell Cohoon Robert Ransom thomas Day Junr William harris John Jonson Clement kithophell Ar-

ther Scofell Benjamin Lewis & Left holms—fence vewers sergt
Ephream foot & samuell brown—Listers James tredway &
Joseph pratt Junr   Colecterors Samll kellogg & Daniell Jones
—at the meeting aforesaid the town voated & granted to the
Reuerent Mr Bulkley for his sallery for the year now almost
past: the sum of eighty pownds In prouision pay as it paseth
Currant (as money) from man to man: or In bills of publick
Credett: further it was voted that the present select men with
Decon Lomis and ensign Nathaniell foot be a Comittie to order
the afairs of the Scoole for the year Insueing: further granted
a rate of thre half penc on the pound on the ratable estate in
our present list to defray the town charges.

Decembr the 10th: 1722 was a town meeting held in Colchester: whearin Micaiell Taintor was chosen town Clerk—
Townsmen, Capt Newton Capt Wright Lef Wyat—Constables
Ensign foot & Noah Wells Ensigne Nathaniell foot Chosen to
gather the Contry Rate and make up the acounbts with the
tresurer acording to Law—Grand Jurymen sergt prat & Benjemin Lewis—Colecterors John Jonson & Samll Lomis Junr—
waywardens John Jonson thomas day Junr Jonathen kellogg
left John holms Left James harris Daniell Jones Benjamin
Lewis Nathanill Cohoon Noah Wells Samll knight James
kinion & Daniell Clark all sworn but Cohoon—Listers James
tredway Joseph pratt Junr—pownd keeper Sergt prat fence
vewers Ephream foot & Samuill Brown—further at the meeting aforesaid mentioned on the opposite side the town voated Mr
Bulkleys sallery for the year now Allmost past the sum of one
hundred pounds in bills of Credett or in prouision pay at the
price that the Contry hath stated—further voated to giue Nathanll kellogg Junr twelve shillings for the year Insuing to
beat the Drum on Sabath Days for meetings—he finding himself a Drum—further at the same meeting the town voated:
to grant a Rate of one penne half penne on the pownd to defray the town Charges—titheing men Sergt Dible Richard

Church—School Comittie Chosen ware the present Select men
& ensign Wells & Micaiell Tantor—further voated that wheras
we formerly voated to give twenty shillings for a woolf we
now Continue yt act for all that are killed in this town bounds
by our own Inhabetents—In addistion to the voat abouesd it is
now voated that if killed by our Inhabetents thay shall be
paid for notwithstanding thair being killed without the town
bounds—this adistion made at the meeting: Decembr 9th 1723

March ye 12th: 1722–3: Was a town meeting held in Colchester—it was voated to seat the meeting hows—Also voated &
agreet yt a Comittie of thre men Shold Do yt seruice & the
Commitie Chosen were Ensign foot Left Skiner & Ensign
Wells—& further voated that the fore or front galery & the
west pues to be equall with the second seat in the body of the
hows—further the upermost seat in the side galery to be equall
with the third seat in the body of the hows—& the other seat
in side galery to be equall with the fowrth seat—the two pues:
next or behind the Dore on the east side: to be the second in
dignety—& the two next pues Joyning to the aforesaid pues to
be equall with the second seat in the body of the hows—further
voated that the Rules in seating shall be acording to the same
Ruels as the former seaters had=to gether with a refferenc
to the thre last rates—further voated that yong men of the
age of twenty one years & maids at eighteen years of age to
be seated—further voated that the Comitie for buelding of the
galleries; shall haue power to Call in thre Workmen to Judg
the work that mr Worthing hath don in buelding the galleries:
in Conjuntion with mr Worthington—further the town voted
& Chose Ensign foot a Comitie to Joyn with mr Bulkley &
Left harris to settell the line or to attend the Comitie which
the Generall Court appoynted to setell the line betwixt norwich & Colchester

at a Legall Town meeting held in Colchester Decembr—
1723—Micaiell Taintor was chosen town Clerk for the year

3

ensuing—Select men Capt. Wright Left skiner & Left holmes
—Constables Ensigne foot & sergt Isaac Jones—Colecterors
John hitchcock & Isaac Biglow—Listers Isreall Newton &
Daniell Clark Grand Jurymen ebenezer kellogg & Richard
Church—Tithingmen Sergt kellogg William Williams &
thomas Day Senr—Way Wardins James tredway James
welch Isack fox Jacob Lomis Jonathan kellogg Nathaniell
Cohoon John Rowlee Thomas Day senr Samull fuller Jabesh
Grippen Noah Wells Joseph pepoon Jonathan Northam sergt
Ephream foot—fenc vewers John Jonson & wm Roberds—
Voated to grant mr bulkley for his sallery one hundred pounds
* * * At the meeting aforesaid the town voated & granted
a rate of one penne on the pound to Defray ye Nesesary
Charges of ye town—further ensign foot & James Tredway
were Chosen to Audet the former acoumlts with the selectmen: so that thare may be an acoumlt layd before the town:
yt is to say—the acoumlts of ye last thre years—further
granted to Decon Lomis seauen shillings pr week for the keeping mr Alison: for ye time past to be paid out of ye town
Rate—further voated that the present Selectmen shall be the
School Comitie—further Voated yt wharas thare is a Certaine
parcell of Comon Land adjoyning to the meeting hows which
hath bin formerly Cleared & staddels left thareon for ye Conueniency of horses: it is now enacted yt notwithstanding any
former act of ye town to ye Contrary: yt all those stáddels or
trees now Remaining: near the bueriing yard & so fifteen
Rods distance rownd from the meeting howse Be Reserued for
that end: & that any perseuering to Cutt Down any tree or
staddell within fifteen Rods of the meeting hows shall forfitt &
pay to ye town tresury the sum of fiue pounds—farther Voated
to fence & clear so much of the buriing yard as may be Conuienient

At a town meeting held in Colchester Aprell the 30th 1723
the town voated to Chose fowr men to be added to the former

Comite in seating the meeting hows & the men Chosen ware
Left harris Sergt prat Decon Lomis & Capt Newton & further it was voated to submit to that which thay shall Do in
that matter & the Rules formerly giuen to be attended ondly
one head to one famely to be considered in all the Rates Relating to the seating—further voated & exsepted of John an-
derson to be an Inhabitant in this town—John nox was also
exsepted an Inhabetant

Decembr ye 14th=1724 was a town meeting held in Col-
chester: Micaiell Taintor was Chosen town Clerk—Selectmen
Capt Wright Left holms & Left Skiner—Constables ensign
Nathll foot & sergt Isaac Jones thay are to gather the Contry
rate equaly to be Conserned in it ensign foot to be returned
to the treasurer to make up ye coumlts (accounts, C. M. T.)
Grand Jurymen Decon Lomis & noah Wels—tithing men
Benjamin Lewis & Daniell Jones—Colecterors ware Jacob
Lomis & John Day—Listers James Newton John wels John
biglow & Noah Clark—fenc vewers ephriam foot & Samuell
brown—way wardens wm Worthington wm Williams Samll
kellogg Isaac biglow Wm Chamberlin Nathll skiner Sergt
thomas Jones & Samll knight William Roberd & Jonathan
Well (s?) Danil Clark—further voated to giue to the Reuerend Mr bulkley for the year now almost past one hundred
pounds in money or prouision as money—Schole Comittie
Chosen ware Insign foot Benjamin Lewis and James newton—
further voated to grant Decon Lomis seauen shillings pr week
for keeping mr Allison for ye time past—further at the meeting aforesd granted to Ebenezer Skiner the liberty of giting
wood to make Cole in the sequestred Comons to maintain
Iron works so long as he shall maintain & keep up the
Iron works—further it was voted & granted a rate of one
penne on the pound to all ye Rateable estate in ye town

aprell ye 27th: 1725 Was a legall Town meeting held in
Colchester—Vpon the petistion of the Inhabetants of the south
east part of said Colchester Desireing the Consent & liberty

to make a parrish; Joyning with ye north part of lyme voated
& granted to set of for the Incoragement of the petistioners to
make a parrish for their more Conuenient attending on ye
worship of god, to set of from the south east part of the town—
as followeth (viz) the line to begin at Sergt thomas Jonses
norwest Corner bounds: & so to Run to sd Jonses noreast
Corner bounds: & thenc to run a Streight line to Labanon
Corner whare Colchester norwich & labanon meet Including
mr thatchers Improuements Into sd parrish, the sd parish &
each Inhabetent Included in yt part of it yt is in Colchester
bounds to Pay thair taxes to ye town sosiety untill thay Call
a minester & pay minesters Rats among them selues: but if
ye sd parrish shall neglect to Continue a minester in the public
seruice of Religion that then thay shall pay thair taxes to the
towns sosiety as formerly—at the meeting aforesd granted to
Capt Joseph Wright Ebenezer Skiner Joseph Dewey & Josiah
Gillett Junr ye liberty of ye stream on Jeremiahs Reuer to
set up Iron works & also the preueleg of fiue or six acers of
land if it be thare to be for a pastuer whare a Conuenient
place is, thay to haue ye priueleg of it so long as thay shall
maintain Ironworks or other mills thare & no longer, the place
lying about 40: or: fifty Rods Down the reuer from James
Roberdses souwest Corner of his home lot—Recorded Apprell
ye 28th 1725—at the meeting aforesd the Return of the following high wais—exscepted and voated & ordered to be recorded, which is as follows * * * * * * * *
    Decembr ye 13: 1725 was a town meeting held in Colches-
ter Micaiell taintor was Chosen town Clerk—Selectmen Capt
Newton Left Wyate & left Skiner Constables Josiah Gillett
Junr & sargt Isaac Jones: Josiah Gillett to gather ye Contry
rate & to make up acoumbt wth ye tresurer—Grand Jury men
Daniell Clark: & Cornelus Roberds—Surueyers Samull brown
Senr asariah Lomis Joseph prat Junr Danill Chamberlin James
kinion Joseph Dalee pelatiah bliss Jonathan Dunham Daniell

Jones and Noah Wells & thomas addams & John Jonson &
John holms & Robert Ransom—fenc Vewers thomas addams
and Samuel knight—Listers John holms John Day Junr &
Joseph Wright Junr—Colectorers Cor-ll Samul lfuller & pelatiah bliss—Tithingmen sergt biglow & Jonathan Northam—
Voated Mr bulkley for his salery one hundred pounds—Choole
Comittie ensign Wells serg Ephream foot Sergt John biglow—
howards Sergt John biglow Sergt ephream foot Isaac biglow
Joseph Dalee Robert Ransom John Jonson Jabesh Rowllee—
granted to Decon Lomis Seauen Shillings per Weeke for his
keeping Mr alleson for the time past—further Voated & granted:
to andrew Carier and Nathaniell Skiner the liberty of the stream
of Jeremiah's reuer : about eight or ten Rods below the mouth
of pine swamp brook : whare it emtieth it self into Jeremis
Reuer, for the setting up a grist mill.

● at a Legall town meeting held in Colchester Decembr 13th
1725 the town being Informed yt ye Generall Court held at
Ncwhauen in october last past : haue granted yt thare shall be
a new County on the east & noreast part of this goverment in
which County Colchester is propounded to be encluded and the
Inhabetants of sd town Conseueing sundry Inconveniences that
may attend thair being anexted thereunto haue unanemusly
agreed : & voated : that aplication shall be made to the honer-
able Generall Court in May next by our Representatives : in
behalf of ye town : that the said town of Colchester may Continue in the County of hartford as formerly—Wharas thare was
a town Voat Decembr 27th : 1720 that swine should go at larg
on the Commons it is now at ye meeting aforesaid : voated yt
ye said voat shall be Repealed & is hearby Repealed and made
void & yt ye law of this Colony : made : at Newhauen : 1720
for Restreigning swine from going on the Comons shall take
place : after the first Day of aprell next ensuing—the meeting
aforesd is adjorned untill the next munday.

The town met together acording to adjornment—then a Co-

mittie was Chosen : namely Sergt John Chapman Sergt Joseph
prat & nathaniel Cohoon : to repair the meeting hows : that is
to say : to prouid Clabords & Clabord the meeting hows anew :
& mend the top of the hows : & also to mend the underpining
of the hows—and sergt John biglow & sergt Isaac Jones ware
added to the sd Comitie—at the meeting aforsaid voated to exchang : with Micaiell Taintor a Corner of his Lot which he
bought of Richard Carrier : & to giue him so much at another.
place as left Skiner : & sergt prat : & left Wyat to mesuer : so
much as is Conuienient for the high way to pass & to giue Satisfaction in land at another place—acording to thair discrestion :
further voated yt thare should be a high way of four Rods wide
Down on the north side of ben smith lot out of the town lot
upon Condistion : that ye persons liueing nigh the sd lane will
make & maintaine ye Cosway ouer the swomp on thair own
Charg & also yt if thare be not 20 acers remaining in ye town
lot : Left Wyat will alow what it wants out of his home lot—
the persons to make & maintain this Cosway are the subscribers namely left Wyat Ensign foot Ebenezer Colman Jonthn
Northam—it is to be understood that thare shall be liberty to
pond the swomp at any time notwithstanding the high way | at
the meeting aforesd granted to James Roberds to take vp ten
acers of land of the town Comons at ye Rear of his & his
father Dayles Deuision he giueing up as much next to the Iron
works, & left Skiner & John Jonson be a Comitie—it was
voated to leaue it with the Comitie.

March ye 18th 1726 : was a Legall town meeting held in
Colchester : Leftent Wyat chosen moderator—Leftent Skiner
& ensign foot Chosen a Comittie to Joyn with a Comittie of ye
new parish to Run & settell the line betwixt that parish & the
town parish which is to be don acording to the voat & grant of
ye town at thair Meeting Aprell 27th 1725.

March 31st : 1726 : was a Legall town meeting held in Colchester & it was voated to Allow to the new sosiatie the one
half of Mr bulkleys Rate which is already Made that is to say

the half of thare Rate (viz) all that is to be paid or is entered to be paid to mr bulkley for the year past of all & euery person belonging to the sd new parrish the whole being about fifteen pounds=9s=& 4d=& the other half to be paid by the Colecteror to Mr bulkley—the town meeting is adjorned untill the freemens meeting in aprell next : which is the last tuesday of Aprell : 1726.

at the town meeting acording to ye Adjornment aboue mentiont it was voated & granted to Raise a Rate of one half penne on ye pound of all the Rateable estat in the town acording to the present list of estates—thar was a town sosiatie meeting at the same time abouesd & it was voated to repair the meeting hows that is to say to mend ye underpininge : & mend ye roof & board ye sets with boards & clabords what is need full for ye present : & sergt ephream foot was apointed to do the work or Cause it to be Don & when it is Don according to the true meaninge of ye voat : that then the present select men to haue power to make a Rate to Defray ye Charg, & said ephream foot was Chosen Colecteror to gather ye sd Rate.

at a Legall town meeting held in Colchester september ye 13th, 1726 it was voated that whereas in december last past thare ware sundry persons Chosen to pound swine going at larg in ye Comons : it is now voated to releas them from that office and that thay shall not be obliged to pound swine more then any other persons—further voated that our Depetue shall make aplycation to the Generall Court in october next for the settelment of the Lyne betwixt hebron & Colchester acording to the agrement made betwixt the Comitties : of the sd towns : & yt ye town of hebron be notified of thair proseading in ys matter.

Nouember 25 : 1726 was a town meetinɡ held in Colchester & by reson of the badnes of the weather the meeting was adjorned untill the next munday : then the meeting was held by sd adjornment at the time aforsd and then it was voated to hire a Schole master for the whole year acording to Law : & to Remoue ye School unto seuerall parts of ye town : to such places as a Comittie shall se Cause—and each place whare ye school is kept shall haue it kept thare so long as thair share of ye Contry money amounts to acording to the lists of thair estates : and the bounds of each place whare ye school is kept to be determined by the Comittie : & Cap Newton Left Skiner Ensign Wells Sergt kellogg & sergt ephream foot ware Chosen a Comittie to manage that Afaire—further at ye same meting granted to the Reuerant mr bulkley about two acers of Land lying at the Rear of his home lot part of which is a pond : to be bounded out by left Skiner surueyr which land Mr bulkley is to haue for the clearing thereof for the term of twenty years next ensueing & no longer, then to be thrown vp to the Comons.

Decembr ye 11th (1726?) was a town meeting held in Colchester—Micaiell Taintor was Chosen town Clerk—Select men Capt Newton Left Skiner William Robord & Lef holms & Daniell Clark—Constabels Josiah Gillet Junr & Isaac Jones—Grand Juremen ensign foot & Daniell Jones — Colecterors sergnt Lewes & Joseph Chapman—Lesters Joseph Chamberlin Junr thomas Day Junr & James harris Junr : Surueyrs Samuell Lomis Junr James Kinion Nathan Williams Samuell knight John Roberds Jeames Roberds Ebenezer Colman Joseph prat Junr George holmes pelatiah bliss sergt thomas Jones Ebenezer kellogg John Rowlee Daniell Chapman Jonathan kellogg Jonathan Dunham—fenc Vewers Noah pumery & Joseph kellogg—pownd keeper sergt prat—howards Samuel Knight Samuel fuller William haris Enathan Rowlce James Kinion Samuel kellogg benjamin quiterfield Jonathan Dunham Joseph Dalec—at the meating aforsd granted to decon lomis 7 shillings per week for keeping mr alleson : to be paid out of ye present town Rate—granted mr bulkley for his salery for the year now almost past one hundred pounds in bills of publick Credet.

at A legall town meeting held in Colchester : Aprell ye 25 : 1727—it was voated and Considered that ye Confining of swine acording to the strictnes of ye law is fownd to be Very Damagefull on sundry acounts therefore it is now agreed & Voated that all swine shall haue liberty within this town belonging to the Inhabetants tharof to Run at Larg acordin to ye Law Intitled an act Conserning sheep & Swine in page 109 : and further voated that ye present howards are Released from thayr office of Impounding swine—further voated that shepe shall go at larg without a keeper this present yeare—further voated that whereas thro a Mistake the highway that was suposed to be Left for Micaiell Taintor Junr to go to his meadow is shut vp by the runing of John Days line that so he hath not any high way to his meadow & also som of his land taken off by sd line : now he prays that the town would grant liberty to thomas Carier that on Condistion sd Carier would throw vp land for a high way thare he may take vp what is taken off from his land for sd high way, in som other place (which is now granted & also granted to sd Taintor liberty to take vp what is taken of from his land in som other Conuenient place—further voated that our deputis Do prosecut our ptistion at the generall Court in may next Relating to the bounds betwixt hebron & Colchester.

at a town meeting held in Colchester October ye 6 1727 it was voated to Impower our deputis to prosecute our petistion at ye Generall asembly in october Instant Relating to the setelment of ye bounds betwixt hebron & Colchester.

Nouember ye 16th : 1727 : was a town meeting held in Colchester : it was then voated to Justefie ye Select men in what thay haue Don in ye Controuersie with mr James tredway : & further to take the Controuersie into thare own hands :—

December ye 11th : 1727—was a town meeting held in Colchester : wharein *Micaiell Taintor* was Chosen town Clerk : Select men Left Wyat noah Wells benjamin Lewes—Constable Josiah Gillett—Grand Jury men William Dickson Joseph pepoon & thomas addams & John Jonson—Colecters of rates phillip Caverly Joseph foot—Listers Benjamin Graues Ebenezer Northam George holms & Nathel kelloogg Junr fenc uewers Sergt Ephream foot & Samuell brown senr—Surueyrs

noah Clark thomas day Junr Daniell worthington Nathll Skiner
William Shamberlin Benjamin fuller Jabez Rowlee James haris
Junr Daniell *p(a)lmeter* arter Scofell Samuell brown senr—
way wardens Isaac fox Daniell Chapman Jonathan kilburn John
hitchcock—tithing men John hitchcock & Samll knight—granted a Rate of a half-penne on ye pound.

at a town meeting held in Colchester December ye 9th 1728.
Micaiell Taintor was Chosen town Clerk for ye yeare ensueing
—Select men Isreall Newton sergt lewes & ensign foot—Con-
stabls Josiah Gillet Junr & Isaac Jones—Grand Jurymen
thomas Addams Jacob Lomis & philep Cauerle—Listers Noah
Wells Samuell fuller & Ebenezer Dible & sergt thomas Jones
—Way wardens Sergt pratt william williams Josiah Gates Jo-
seph brown ebenezer Colman William brown John Chapman
Jonathan kellogg Benjamin quierfield (Cithophell or Quithi-
field, o. m. t.) William Chamberlin Joseph Chamberlin wm
Chapman Junr James kinyon Caleb Lomis—fenc vewers John
Jonson & Noah Clark—at the meeting aforsd it was vooted yt
thare should be a high way Laid out from the north Meadow
up to ye Corner tree to ye line yt mr kemberly Run.

December ye 14th 1730 was a town meeting in Colchester—
Micaiell Taintor was Chosen town Clerk—ensign foot moderator—Select men ensign foot sir John bulkley & ebenezer kellog—Gran Jury men Mr otis & Joseph prat Junr Constabls
Joseph chamberlin & Isaac Jones—Listers (names in a different
hand, o. m. t.) Benjm Chamberlin Benjam Quitefield James
Treadway Joshua Duglis Caleb Loomis) Surueyrs Daniell Jones
palatiah bles Joseph foot James Croker Noah Colman Stephen
brainard Nathaniell Skiner Junr Georg holms Arther scophell
& Sergt Dible Daniell Chapman—fenc vewers John Northam
& thomas Day—at the meeting aforsd granted a rate of one
half-penne on ye pound—Colecters chosen wear Robert Ransom & John Clark.

At a town meetinge held in Colchester Janewary 21: 1702
it was granted to giue to ye Reuerd Mr John Bulkley forty

pownds as mony for his incoragement in ye worke of ye Minestry this yeare & to pay him 10 £ at ye end of every quarter
—further at ye meetinge aforesd was granted to Ebenezer Dibell so much vpland joyning unto ye swamp formerly Granted
to him in Lew of meadow to make up his full proportion of
meadow—At ye same meetinge Micaiell Taintor senr was chosen
towne clerk—further it was Granted to thomas skiner and his
son Ben: Skiner Samll fuller Micaiell Taintor senr & Micaiell
Taintor Juner the littell Round meadow lying west from ye
town with ye swomps : ye swomps to be acounted two acers for
one of meadow : so much as to make up their 1sɟ Deuision of
meadow exsepting if ye towne see cause to take a pece for Clay
they are to lay it out within one yeare & to make recompence
elcwhare—further granted to Samuell Gilbert Samuell Northam
Jonathan Northam, James Brown James mun Jonathan kilburn
John adams Junr & John bacor the long meadow : to haue their
proportion of meadow in equall proportion with others—further
Granted to William Roberts senr His proportion of meadow by
John Days meadow at ye wigwam swomp—further granted to
Samuell Lomis Charles Williams Joseph prat Thomas Day
Ebenezer Coleman Daniel Clark & Andrew Carier the meadow
called nonesuch & one acer of swomp to ye hundred pownd lotment in consideration of ye remotenes of it—further it was
granted to John bacor a home lott on the south side of Clem-
ence Cithophells home lott—further granted to Samuell fuller
his first Devision of upland at ye mouth of ye brook That
Cometh out of ye littell rownd meadow & to run by the great
Brook yt Cometh out of Stebbinses meadow—at ye meeting
aforesd granted to John Adams Junr his 1st Deuision of vpland
next to Joseph pumerys Deuision southward Next Southward
to Samuell Gilbert Next Southward to Jonathan Kilburn Next
Southward to John Brown.

at a Legall town meeting held in Colchester Decemb: 25th
1710 Micaiell Taintor chosen town Clerk for ye year insuing—
Select men chosen ware left–t Weles Decon Lomis & Micaiell

Taintor—Constabels Chosen ware Nathaniell foot & Micaiell
Taintor Junr—to gather Contry rate Micaiell taintor ondly conserned—listers ware chosen : ebenezer Dibell Josiah strong : &
Noah weles Junr—Way wardens Nathll kellog: charles williams—& mr John huberd chosen way warden southward from
ye deepe reuer & so to call out the inhabetentc liueing on that
side the said reuer to work as ocation shall be—at the meeting
aforesaid the towne granted a rate of thre pence on the pownd
in Currant pay as mony & Joseph chamberlin & ebenezer Colman Colecterers to gather sd rate & make up acounts with the
townsmen with the twelue penne rate formerly granted that
thay ware also Colecterors for—Daniell Clark Junr & ephream
foot chosen Colecterors to gather the minesters Rate: fenc
vewers ware chosen: namely Noah Colman Samuell pellett—
at the meeting aforesaid the towne granted the Reuerent mr
bulkleys Rate for this yeare insueing to be fiuety pownds to be
payd in wheat at fowr shillings per busshell indian corn at two
shillings per bushell or mony—further granted to him all the
mony that Major leueston oweth to the town—further the town
voated to impower the townsmen to hire a person or persons to
prouide & bring Mr bulkley his wood for this year insuing at
fowr shillings a cord to be payd out of the town rate—at the
same meeting Joseph Chamberlin was chosen ordynary keeper:
further voated to hire mr pennok or any other person to keepe
school & the townsmen to agre with him or any other—at the
meeting abouesd was granted to John hubbord thre hundred
acres of land on the west side of the great pond southerly from
peter masons howse—further granted to J- bebee to remoue the
bounds of his farm further northward so as to bring the whole
or part into Colchester bounds—further voated that if the Co-
mitty mr woodbridge & the rest com to Colchester to isue our
diference about our land before the next town meeting it shall
be acounted legall for so many of the inhabetentc of Colchester as shall apear to treat with them to haue power to agre

with them or to do & act what they Judg needfull in that matter.

June 27 : 1705—Colchester—whearas I haue right by purchass to fowr hundred Acers of meadow & upland adjoyning to ye land called Stebinses land on the east side of the town platt of Colchester begineng at ye brow of the hill called Chepiantup hill one mile in length north & south a line parellell with Stibins his land & is all that land & meadow in bredth east & west between the land formerly John posts of norwich & now leftenent John huffs of newlondon I protest against any record made of any part thereof & by these enter Cauett : John prentice.

Jenewary ye 10th : 1714–15 : John prents abouesaid renewed his Cauett abouesaid :

Colchester June 27 : 1705 whearas I haue a deed of gift from John post of Norwich for one hundred & thirty acers of upland & meadow in partnership with one hundred & thirty acers yet in the hands of John post which Land & meadow lyeth on the deepe brooke easterly from Colchester town & begins at an old Beuer dam called wecachoweg & runeth westerly 3 hundred & eighty rods to land & meadow claimed by Captin John prentice : & in bredth one hundred rods I protest against any record made of any part therof & by these enter Cauete : John hough.

At a legall Town meeting held in Colchester December ye 13th : 1709—Micaiell Taintor chosen town clerk—townsmen chosen ware Samuell Northam Decon Lomis & Micaiell Taintor—Constabels chosen ware Joseph Dewey & Micaiell Taintor Junr—Way wardens chosen & sworn ware Left Weles & ebenezer Coleman & thomas Day—fence vewers Joseph prat & Nathaniel foot—Colecterors Joseph Chamberlin & ebenezer Coleman—Listers Sergt noah Coleman Sargt John skiner & Corpll Nathaniell kellogg—howards Medad pumery & Jonathan Gillett—at the meeting afore sd it was agreed on & voated

4

that for the feuture mr bulkleys salery shall be raised yearly in Jeneware and the year to begin on the first of Jeneware next from this Date & for this present year to pay him from the first of march last past unto the first of Jeneware next: deducting what time he hath bin absent on the Country seruice—further it was voated to Grant mr bulkleys salery this present year to be after the rate of fiuety pownds as mony—further at the same meeting the town voated to hire the present schoolmaster namely James pennock to keep school with what he hath already kept the term of half a year & to pay him fiueteen pownd in that way & maner as the law directs—at the meeting aforesd granted to decon Skiner to exchang about one acer of Land of his second deuision for Conuenienc of beuldings—at the same meeting granted to Charles williams liberty to bring up his sec-ond deuision land to Joyne on moudus Rhoad & to leaue out as many acers as he takes at the rear of sd deuision—at the meet-ing aforesaid the town voated to exschang with Joseph wright so many rods of land at the Corner of the home lot which was formerly James taylors we say as much as the present towns-men Judg Conuenient & to lay him out dubell to what they take of from sd Corner out of the Comons on the side of sd lot —further at the meeting aforesaid the town sold the old meet-ing hows to ebenezer Coleman for eight pownds to be payd in nailes at mony price ondly Reserueing the boards of the floor & all other loose bords & the pulpitt.

At A Legall Town meeting held in Colchester September 6th 1703: The Town being informed that Major palmes Hath or was about to sell A parsell of land within ye township of Cole-chester under a pretence of an Indian grant—Namely Capt Sannap ye town Considering that trobell may Arise in that matter do hearby impower Joseph pumery & ebenezer Coleman to eject the said Major palmes or any other person that shall make enteranc or improue any land in the bounds of Colches-ter without ye aprobation of the town & for their incoragment the town do grant to them ye said Joseph pumery & ebenezer

Coleman eaeh of them one hundred akers of land at A placo on which they haue Aready Made enteranc by fencing about seauen Miles from our town plat at or near paugunk prouided thay stand to defend ye land that Major palmes or any other person or persons shall Make enteranc upon in right of Capt Sanap: it is to be understood that thay shall defend it at thair own Charg & to ye outermost exstent of law:—

at a legall town meting held at Colchester July 26: 1703 it was voated to enter on record one home lott which was formerly granted to John Stebbins but not then entered—it is ye lott lying North from John adamses sener his home lot.

Lebanon June ye 17th 1703 then receaved of Joseph pomry of Colchester fiue pownds & Ten Shilings in Corrent mony on ye acoult (account, c. m. t.) of ye Commitie of Colchester to pay for Beuldinge mr bucklys chimies (chimneys, c. m. t.) I say recvd by me John Woodward.

att ye meting aforesd it was granted yt James Taylor should haue an addistion of one hundred pownds right he payinge ye charge: & it is to be understood yt it is in right of his father in law Daniel stebins & to take it without meadow and ye abouesd Daniel stebins agreeth not to haue any further deuisions of lands in Colchester untill euery hundred pownds lotment hath had one hundred & fifty acers.

att a legall Town meeting held in Colchester September ye 6th 1703 it was granted to william roberts a home lott & other acomadations: exsepting meadow he paying charges as otliers of ye town haue done—at ye meetinge aforesaid it was granted to ebenezer Colman an adistion to his deuision land 3 acers for one yt he wants in his home lot— * * * *" (Next follows an entry in an unknown hand, by some one who was chosen Clerk pro tem., viz.:)

"att a Legall towen meeting held in coltchester November the 29=1703 then it was voted and granted vnto Iserall wiatt an alotment and vnto Samvell allis an alotmen with the Liberty of tow Strems to Bvlde (build, c. m. t.) a grist mill and a Saw mill provided thay Bvlde the mills forthwith and mayntayn them from tim to time for the towens yovs (use, c. m. t.) and allso thar is granted vnto them 60 acers of Land to Ly to the grest mill Bvt when thay lett the milles fall the strems shall Retvrn to the towen agayn—thay are allso obliged to sell thar Bordes a 22 shilings pvr thovsand from tim to time and at all · times for ever."   (Here ends the entry by the Clerk pro tem.)

At a town meeting held in Colchester december 29: 1703— Thomas Skiner was chosen Constabell for ye year insuinge & Micaiell Taintor was chosen town Clerk for ye yeare insuinge —Thomas Day Joseph wright & Micaiell Taintor Chosen townsmen for ye year insuing—Joseph pratt was chosen way-warden—Joseph wright was Chosen brander for ye town—John chapman & John hopson Chosen fenc vewers—at ye meeting aforesd granted to Samull Lomis his 1st Deuision of meadow lyinge on ye east side of Stebinses meadow against ye front of Nathanll foots lott exscpting a high way: Nextly granted to thomas Day ye meadow formerly Granted to Samill belding in Stebinses meadow—Nextly granted to Joseph prat yt meadow yt ebenezer Dibell mowed this yeare lying north of lebanon road on ye great brook: & thare to haue his 1st Deuision—Nextly granted to Daniell Clark twelve acers of upland lyinge Joyn-inge northward to his 1t Deuision which is in ye lew of his 1t deuision of meadow.

At ye meetinge aforesd viz. December 29: 1703 Granted to william roberts his 1t Deuision of upland on the north side of Samull Northams Deuision—Nextly granted unto thomas sel-din & Jonathan ingram each of them one hundred pownd lot-ment exsepting meadow & thay are to pay each of them fiue pownds in mony & to Com & settell heare spedyly: further it was voated & Declared yt ye lott Granted to thomas Day of hartford to be forfit to the towne—& also ye lott Granted to Samull beldin to be forfitt—further Granted to John Kilbvrn

one hundred pd lotmt he payinge fiue pownds & settell spedily
on it.

At a legall Towne meeting in Colchester febr 17th 1703-4
it was granted that ye reurend Mr John bulkly his sallery shall
be for ye year insuing forty pownds as mony—further it was
voated yt Joseph pratt & John Skener shold lay out ye town
highwaise—further granted to John waters his 2d Deuision * *
further granted to John addams his 2d Deuision * * * * further granted unto moses rowley his deuision of upland on ye
south side of the way which leads to modus & on ye east side
of Charles williams his deuision—further granted to noah Coleman a lott & acomadations amongst us to a two hundred pd
right exsepting meadow prouided he pay ten pownds in mony
& Com & settell here within thre months henc—further at ye
meeting aforesd granted unto Samuell pelit a homelot & a hundred pownds right he payinge fiue pownds & settell amongst us—
at ye meetinge aforesd granted unto micaiell Taintor Sener yt
parsell of land which lyeth between his 2d Deuision & ye great
brook & to go down ye brook to ye place where ye Cart way
now is & to run upon the ledg of rocks westward he alowing so
much as there is in his next deuision—further granted unto
Nathanell Kelogg what he wants of his 2d Deuision on ye south
side of lebanon road—farther it was voated yt all inclosures of
homelots or elcewhare shall be fenced so as to be Judged sufis-
ient by ye fenc vewers & no swine powndabell untill ye fenc
be so ajudged: .

At a town meetinge held in Colchester March 16th 1703-4
was granted to Samuell pellet his 1 dcuision next to his home
lot on ye west side of lime road about 2 miles from ye towne—
at ye meetinge aforesd receaued from Samull waler under his
hand: yt he doth grant to ebenezer Killogg all his right of land
in Colchester: & ye towne uoated to exsept of ebenezer kellogg
an inhabetent in ye Towne & grant him a home lott upon ye
right aforesd—further granted to natheniell kelogg & Samull

pellit liberty to set up a saw mill on ye brook Caled ye gouern-
ers Brook & thay to haue ye streame so long as thay maintaine
a sawmill thare: & to haue it goinge at or before ye last of September next—further voated yt all such persons as haue lots
heare in Colchester shall Com & Dwell with us in a Constant
Way: & in Defalt thareof to forfitt thair right in ye Towne.

At a town meeting held at Colchester aprell 24: 1704—it
was granted to mr John bulkley a swamp which Joyns to his
home lot on ye north side be it one acer more or les—at a meeting aforesd granted to ebenezer kalog twenty acers for his home
lot & 30 acers for his next deuision * * * * in right of Samuell walers—at the meting aforesd mentioned on ye other side
granted unto Isreall Wiatt that lot lyinge on ye south side of
Joshua Whelers for his home lott: further granted to Isreall
wiatt aforesd his next Deuision of land with twenty acers on ye
acount of ye mill grant of land betwene ye two east meadows—
further granted unto isreall wiatt a parsell of meadow lyinge
betwene James browns meadow & micaiell Tantors—further
granted unto william lord one hundred pownd Lotment prouided
he pay fiue pownds & settell forthwith.

At a legall town meeting held in Colchester July ye 3d 1704
granted unto John Chapman his 1t deuision of upland at the
west side of new london road where norage road goeth across
lime road he relinquishing his former grant—further granted
unto John·polie a home lott on the south side of John bacors
lott with a two hundred pownd right he payinge charges equall
with us & beuld a sawmill with all conuenient speede & settell
amongst us :"

(Next is an entry in the hand of Capt. Joseph Wright, who
was Clerk pro tem., viz.:)

„Att A Legall Town Meeting Holdn in Colchestr octob.r 30:
1704 it was voted that Mr Micha Tainter & Joseph Wright
should Treat with Jno Poley in Regard of his bulding A saw
Mill & Demand an Evidence of his Ability & also satisfie them
that he will acomplish it by the Time the Town intend.d in their

Grant to him, & if he Cannot to make A tender to him of the
said former Grant att teen pounds as is vsuall to others : Att
the Town Meeating aforesd it was voted that Every man poses-
ing A two Hundred pound Right, shall Bring for the Rev.d Mr
Bulkley A Cord of Wood & Cord it att His house & thos of A
hundred pound Right to Doe half so much : with in the space
of one Moneth upon penalty of forfiting five shillings—Att the
Town Meeting aforesd it was voated that Evin Joans should
have A Grant of Teen Acres for A home lot att the Est side
of Tho Browns home Lot if there be Roome for it there & if
not to have it as Convenient as may be one the Contrary side
of the highway—At the Meeting aforesd it was Grantd that
Jno Baker should have an Iseland of vpLand lying in Compase
wt his Meadow he Releseing to the Town as much in his next
Devision : Att the Meating afore sd it was Granted that Noah
Coleman should have twenty Acres of Land in a flaig swomp
Lying at the south End of the Est medow in Consideration of
his Medow—Att the Meeating aforesd it was Grantd that
Willm Robards Junr should have five Acres Lying Next to his
teen Acres Grantd for Medow which five Acres was Due to
his father from the Town—Att the Meating aforesd it was
Granted to Iserel Wyatt that he should have A piece of medow
Lying att Nonesuch begining att that point of the medow Next
to Machamoodus Rhoad & to Extend southward toward the
main Medow so far as to make up his Due of Medow if there
be a sufisiensi—Att the Meeting afores.d it was voted that those
persons that have not taken up their first Division of Vpland
shall Conclude before the next Town Meeting where to take
up the same : & it is allso voted that att the Next town meeting
the severall Inhabitants shall Draw Lotts for their next or
second Division att one hundred Acres to A two hundred pound
Rite & so proportionably—Att the Meeting afores.d it was
voated & Declared the Lott formerly Granted to ye Honourd
Gouerner to be forfit to the Town." (Here ends the recording
of Capt. Joseph Wright, clerk pro tem. c. m. t.)

"At a towne meetinge held in Colchester Decembr 18th 1704: Micaiell Taintor Sener was Chosen Clerk for ye yeare insueing—Josiah Gillett Sener was Chosen Constable—Townsmen Chosen Samuell Northam Thomas Skiner Micaiell Taintor Senr—Way wardens Nathaniell kalodg Richard Skiner—fenc vewers Josiah strong Andrew Carier—At ye meeting aforesad granted yt mr eliots & John ingrams first Deuisions of land to be on ye west side of the littell meadow—further granted unto Joseph Chamberlin twenty acers of upland for his medow if it be on ye wigwom hill after Jer. adams his two lotments are layd out—further Granted unto Thomas brown his share of meadow in the long meadow if it be thare after others that haue their Grants thare are suplied—further it was voated & Micaiell Taintor & Joseph pomry were chosen to run the bounds with our Neighboring towns—at the meting aforesd the town proseeded to draw Lots acording to the voate october 30th: 1704.

At the meeting Aprell 12 : 1705 it was voated that all timber & stone shall be fre for any person to git throout the whole township on all lands untill it be inclosed the homelots only exsepted: we say all fire wood timber & stone shall be fre to euery person as aforesd of ye town of Colchester exsept such as now enter a protest against this voate—John Day Joseph prat Deacon Skiner James tayler enter a protest against the aboue voate: At the meeting aforesaid it was granted unto Josiah Gillett Sener fowr acers of land at the south end of his meadow prouided he the said Gillett procure a Good new drum for the use of the towne within one Month after this voat: At the Meeting Aforesaid it was Voated to Grant to Edward woolf of lime one hundred pownd right in the towne & a streame to set up a saw mill prouided he haue the Mill finished At or before the last of October next & settell eighther himself or his son in the town—at the same meeting Micaiell Taintor was voated to keepe ordinary.

at a town meetinge held in Colchester June 26t 1706—the

towne voated to raize a rate to procure a towne stock of powder
our yousiall way of raeting the same to be set at the discrestion of the select men: at the same meeting it was voated to
giue mr John bulkley a deed of his hows & the present select
men are hearby Impowered to giue said deed in behalf of the
town.

At a Legall Town meeting held in Colchester Nouember the
4th 1706 the town granted unto human hinsdell twenty Akers
of land to be laid out on the side of the hill south from the littell brook next southward from the brook Commonly Called
fawn brook & so far on the north side of sd brook as to Com
to the ledg of rocks: further the towne voated & granted unto
Joseph Dewey the home lot & the other acomadations belonging to it which is one hundred pownd right: on Condistion
that he sd dewey pay to the town ten pownds in Mony & also
beuld a fulling mill sometime before the last of May next fitt
for seruice & to maintain sd mill in good repaire & to full cloth
as cheap as any other mill in the colonie—& to settell an inhabitant such as the town exsept on sd lot within one yeare from
this date—it is to be understood yt the lot Granted to Joseph
Dewey on the other side was the lot formerly Granted vnto
Jonathan Ingram—further it is to be understood that if sd
Dewey failes in the premeses Mentioned on the other side then
the sd lotments to return to ye town—further the town Granted
sd Dewey the liberty of the stream yt Coms out of the north
Meadow so long as he Maintains a suffiscient fulling Mill on it
& no longer—further Granted unto James brown a peece of
Land lyinge betwene Jonathan kilburns land & John Cloathers
land: & to take it in part of his hundred akers—further
Granted unto Martin kaalog one hundred pownd right of land
in the town he paying five pownds in mony to ye town & Com
& settell in the town with all Conuenient speed.

febrewary 7th: 1706–7 was a town meeting & then voated
that & Granted that Noah welles shold haue fiuety akers of Land

Joyning to his land at parrum the said fiuety akers is ten akers of it for his meadow & ten akers of it for his half home lot & thirty akers for his 1t Deuision—further voated that ephream foot shold haue sixty Akers of land wher he se cause to take it prouided he the sd foot Com & set vp his trade of a black smith & spedily settell amongst vs—at the same meeting Samull pellet was chosen land mesurcr—Layd out in the yeare 1705 pr John Skiner surer (surveyor, c. m. t.) for Joseph pumery & ebenezer Coleman two hundred akers of land at a place Comonly known by the Name of paugquonk & lyeth bownded as foloweth * * * *

A Town meeting held in Colchester December ye 30th 1706 —Micaiell Taintor was chosen town Clerk for the yeare insueing—Samuell pellett was chosen Constabell & Colecteror—Select Men Deacon Lomis Joseph Chamberlin Micaiell Taintor —fenc vewers Benjamin Skiner Jonathan Northam—Waywardens John Chapman Josiah Strong—At the Meeting aforesaid the town voated to Grant the reurend Mr Bulkleys sallery or Rate to be fiuety pownds in Mony or prouision pay as mony and also that euery hundred pownd Right in the town to pay half a Cord of fire wood to be Brought to mr bulkleys at or before the last of Jenewary Next & euery person neglecting to prouide his proportion of firewood acording to his right in the towne at the time Abouesaid thare shall be added to his Minesters Rate two shillings & six penc to the hundred: which shall be Gathered with ye Rest by the Colecterer—At the Same Meeting Daniell Clark was Chosen Brander this year—At the aforesd meeting the town granted unto Samell pellet the libertie to take up thirty akers of land by John bakers Deuision which is to be part of John Dayes hundred aker Deuision prouided John Day alow of it—further the town voated yt swine shall Go at large & no Damnag don by swine shall be recouerabell exsept it be don in fields that are fenced acording to law:

Joseph Wright hath By purchas of James mun all ye unde-uided Land Belonging to ye sd James mun in Colchester which belongs to a two hundred pound Right part of which is already Drawn for & is in number 3 ye Libertie of ye Comons ondly exsepted for which ye sd James mun hath Giuen a Deed Dated february ye 11t. 1707–8 : & acknoleged before Micaiell Taintor Justice of peac—entered february 24th : 1707–8.

Joseph wright hath purchased of Daniell Clark all the un-deuided Land in Colchester Belonging to sd Daniell Clark for or to one hundred pound Right part of which is Already Drawn for and is in Number (blank, c. m. t.) the Libertie of the Comons ondly exsepted for which ye sd Daniell Clark hath Giuen a Deed Dated Nouembr 13th : 1707 & acknoleged the same Day Before Micaiell Taintor Justice of peac.

At a Legall town meeting held in Colechester Aprell 15 : 1707—the town voated to Repaire the meeting hows with floors & seats & galleries windows & sealing & pulpitt & De-con Skiner Joseph prat & Charles williams ware Chosen a Commitie to Carie on the work—further voated to sequester all the lands on the east side of the town from hebron bounds & lebanon bounds & to exstend southward to Norwich Road & the deep Reuer exsepting any that haue not taken up thair second Deuision : Notwithstanding this voat haue liberty with-in these bounds also the chesnot hill neer the deepe brook is reserued from this sequestration all the Rest to Remain to be town Commons for euer to the present proprietors of Colches-ter & thair sucksesors—further at the Meeting aforesaid the town did sequester on the west side of the town from the north end of the long pond & Joyning on haddam bounds till it Com to pine swomp brook & so Joyning on the brook till it Com to Jeremiahs Reuer & then to bound on hebron bounds till it Com to the aboue mentioned land only exsepting what is want-ing in Second Deuision land as abouesd—all the rest to Remaine town Comons for euer as abouesd—further the town Chose the

Reurend mr John bulkley & Micaiell Tantor to mannage the publick Conserns of the town at the Next generall Court at hartford.

October 13 : 1707 was a towne meeting held in Colchester then voated to Lay out the land that lyeth Joyning to lime bounds & haddam bounds & norwich bounds to be layd 80 akers to a two hundred pownd right & 40 to a hundred pownd right: to each propriator acording as his name is fixed in the number: to ye Draught made in febrewary 7th: 1706-7—at the same meeting voated & Granted to mr James Rogers the son of James Rogers of Newlondon to haue eighty akers of land in the Deuisions aboue to be layd out & to be in the Draught the number of 48: Mr James Rogers abouesd Capt gilbert Joahn Chapman & John skiner ware chosen to lay out the Deuisions abouesd—further at the same meeting granted to Nathaniell lomis to haue a deuision of forty akers with the aboue deuisions & to be the last in Number—further granted to Capt gilbert the liberty to fenc the burieing yard it being two akers & to haue the grase as feed that is on it so longe as he mantains the fenc sufiscent.

Decembr 25th: 1707 was a towne meeting & at ye same Meeting Micaiell Taintor was chosen town Clerk : : ebenezar Coleman was chosen Constabell & Colecterer for this year insuing & sworn—Townsmen Chosen Joseph wright Nathaniell Lomis & Micaiell Taintor senr—way wardens ware Chosen : namely John chapman & Josiah strong—fence vewers ware thomas brown Samuell kalogg william Roberds Juner & John waters Joseph chamberlin was chosen sealer of Leather—Micaiell Taintor was chosen sealer of waights & measurs—at the meeting aforesaid it was granted that mr bulkleys sallerey shold be this year fiuety pownds to be payd as mony in prouision pay as it [is stated in the Country rate exsepting that euery hundred pound Right to pay 1s—6d in siluer mony : & for his fire wood to be prouided as it was the last year.

At a Legall town Meeting held in Colchester March 22d:
1708 the town exsepted of the Return of the steering or Runing the Line dun by william Clark & John Spreag for labanon:
& John Skiner & Joseph prat for Colchester as thay haue
marked out sd bounds betwene the sd towns & haue giuen it
under thare hands in an instrument Dated aprell 25th: 1707:
& that sd instrument shall be entered on Record—further at
the same meeting it was voted that whereas the town street
from the east Corner of Daniell Clarks lot to the North end of
the town plat was formerly agred upon & layd out twelue Rods
in bredth : that is shall be & Remain to be that bredth for euer
—further it was voated that from the west Corner of Joseph
Wrights lot which was formerly James taylers to the lane or
highway that is betwixt Samull Lomises lot & Nathaniell Lomises lot the street to be nine Rods in bredth & from that out-
lot southward to the end of the town plat or home lots to be
twelue Rods & to remaine to be so for euer—& the outlet betwixt Samuel & Nathaniell Lomises lots to be six Rods throu-
ougt to the end of thair home lots & so to be for euer—at the
meeting abouesaid it was voated that the Draught for lots Made
febrewary 7th, 1706–7 should be 100 akers to a two hundred
pownd Right & 50 to a hundred & the first in Number to take
first & so sucksesiuely & after the first of may next all haue
liberty alike.

at a town meeting held in Colchester aprell the 9th: 1708—
the town granted to Capt. John leusston two hundred acers of
Land on the hill west from peter masons hows on the acoumbt
of a former grant of a lotment to our late gourner wintrup he
said leunston paying all Rates that hath bin Raised in time
past equall to a two hundred pownd Right & also for time to
com to bare an equel charg acordingly & also to make present
improument—at the meeting aforesd it was granted to those
that do set up Iron works in the township of Colechester one
hundred & twenty akers of Land & a stream : on Condistion

that the iron works be set up within two full years from the date hearof.

At a legall town meeting held in Colchester Aprell the 27th: 1708 then voated to alow two penc for eury Ratell Snak that shall Be killed any time betwene this Date and ye Midell of may next & so to alow for those that haue bin killed thiss spring: & those that do kill any shall euedenc it to one of the townsmen:—further at the meeting aforesd the town Granted To mr. Richard Edwards one hundred & fiuety acers of Land he paying charges past & to com proportionall to other former grants—further at the same meeting the town granted to noah Wels two triangell pieces of land of about twelue acers Joyning to his own land in Consideration that the Country Rhoad is layd out thro his land about one hundred & twenty Rods——at the meeting aforesd the towne Voated to pay one penne a head for blackbirds that are killed from thiss time untill the last of September next—

at A legall Town meeting held in Colchester June the 11th: 1708 the towne voated to beuld a New meeting hows with all Conuenient speed the length to be forty foots & the bredth to be thirty & six foots with a slatt Roufe—further the town chose Samll Northam Decon Skiner Joseph wright Joseph Pratt & Nathaniell lomis a Comitie to Carie on the beulding & finishing the sd Meeting howse—further the town voated that thare shold be a Rate made to the sum of eighty pounds to carie on & defray ye charg & euery one may pay his part in work as he Can agre with the Comitie—at the meeting aforesd Joseph Pumery Joseph Wright & noah weles were chosen listers for this yeare—further at the same meeting Samell Northam Decon Samell Lomis Joseph wright & ebenezer Coleman were chosen & impowered by the town to sue or eject any person or persons that shall make any enteranc to improue any land within the township of Colchester without liberty from the towne.

at a town meeting held in Colchester Aust the 30: 1709:
the town voated that the eighty pownds aboue mentioned with
that which the generall Court gaue us last October shold be
raysed by the next list of estats now in this year 1709—further the town voated forthwith to raise eighteen penc mony on
a hundred pownd right: for the Carieng on our law suets—
ebenezer Coleman & Joseph Dewey ware Chosen Colectorers
for the gathering sd rate—

at a town meeting held in Colchester Jenewary ye 15:
1710=11 the towne voated to null & make voyd the aboue
Record to John hopson as not being orderly dun—further
voated that wheras John hopson & ebenezer Skiner had a grant
of fiue acres apeac of meadow in the north meadow the grant
not to be found the town now grant the same to them—

at a legall town meeting held in Colchester Decembr ye 31:
1711—Micaiell Taintor was chosen town clerk for the year
insewing—townsmen chosen ware Decon Lomis Joseph wright
& Micaiell Taintor—Constables Chosen ware Nathaniell Foot
serg Joseph pratt—Colecterers ware Nathall Kelloog & Josiah geilet Junr—Listers Chosen ware ensigne wyat Samuell
Pellet & Josiah Gates—way wardens or surueyers ware Daniell Clark Senr Nathaniell Lomis & James brown ebenezer
Dibell & william Roberds Junr—fenc vewers ware Jonathan
Kellogg Josiah phelps—peramelators ware Joseph wright John
Skiner & sergt Rowlee which sd Joseph wright Scrgnt Rowlee
& John Skiner are apoynted a Comitte to setell the bownds
betwene Colchester & Middelltown & haddam: & if any one
of the aboue named Comittie faill the attendanc of that seruice
Samuell pellet is chosen to attend that work in the Room of
him that fails—at the meeting aforesaid the towne voated &
granted to the Reuerant Mr bulkley for his salery the year now
past the sum of fiuety & fiue pownd in mony or wheat at 4s
pr bushell indian Corn at 2s pr bushell—& merchantab: pork
at 2½d pr pownd—at the meeting aforesaid the towne granted

to James brown Nathanill gilbert—Isaac Rowlee & Benjamin fox the liberty of setting up a Sawmill on the long meadow
brook & to haue the liberty of that stream so long as they
maintain a sawmill thare in good repaire prouided it be no
prejudis to any perticqlor person—further the town granted to
James treadway thre acers of land Joyning or neare to his
own land to be layd out at the discrestion of the towne sur-
uaier—further at the meeting aforesaid the town voated to ad
fiue pownds to the fiuety & fiue pownds aboue granted to mr
bulkley for his salery the yeare past—

at a town meeting held in Colchester March the 4th: 1712
—the towne granted to the Reuerant mr bulkley sixty & five
pownds as mony for his sallery this yeare he finding himself
firewood—further the towne voated to add to mr bulkleys
salery yearly for the next fiue years after the first Day of Jen-
eary next from the aboue Date eigt pownds as mony on the
Consideration that he find himself fire wood the sd fiue years:
& Continue in the work of the minestry amongst vs—at the
meetinge aforesaid the towne voated to be at equall Chrg with
midell towne to hire the County Surueyer to setell the bounds
betwixt midelltowne & Colchester—at the same meeting the
towne granted unto Robert Ransom to take up about half an
acre of land for Conuenience of beulding: he leaueing out so
much of his own land to the comons—

"July the 12th: 1705" At a legall towne meetinge in Colchester was granted unto Charels hill eighty akers of land for &
on the a count of his being partner with John stebins & Danell
stebins & the rest of those that agreed with the towne & gaue up
to the town thair Claime: twenty acers of which was for his
home lott—at the meetinge aforesaid granted unto John stebins
sixty akers of upland at the north end of the long pond by the
Coue that runs into the pond: which is to make him equall to
the rest of the proprietors of Colchester in thair last dragft of
lots: at the meeting aforesaid Joseph pomery & thomas day were

chosen to lay out conuenient high ways to ye mill and an outlet or high way ouer the mill brook west: at the meeting aforesaid granted to Isreall Wiatt all the land that lyeth on the
north side of the Cart path that goeth ouer the mill brook into
Micaiell Taintors deuision the town reseruing the land of the
millpond & the round hill by the mill on the east side & also
conuenient highways to the mill & ouer the brook & up on to
ye hill westward—At the meeting afore sayd was further
granted unto John stebins twenty akers to be aded & Joyned
to the sixty akers of land aboue mentioned: which said twenty
akers is granted to make up what he wants to make up his
meadow ten akers for which said stebins declared himself fully
satisfied—

At a town meeting held in Colchester Decembr 30: 1705—
Micaiell Taintor senr was chosen town Clerk for the yeare insuing: & John addams senr was Chosen Constab. for the year
insuinge & sworn—selectmen chosen serjent rowlee Joseph
Chamberlin John Skiner—fence vewers benjamin Skiner Jonathan Northam—way wardens Noah Coleman ebenezer kelogg
—At the meetinge Aforesaid it was voated & declared that
Moses Rowlee hath forfitted his lotments in Colchester to the
towne—At the meetinge aforesaid the towne voated to grant
to the Reuerent Mr bulkley 50 pownds in Mony or prouision
as mony for the year past for his sallery: & that euery person
that hath a two hundred pownd right to bringe Mr bulkley one
Cord of fire wood & one hundred pownd right to bring half a
Cord—All to be brought at or before the last of Jenewary
next; & whomsoeuer shall neglect to do it by that time there
shall be added to his minesters rate two shillings & six pence
to the hundred which the Colecteror shall gather with the rest
—At the meetinge aforesaid Joseph Wright & Joseph pratt
ware Chosen to run the bownds betwene labanon & us & also
betwene haddum & us—At the meeting aforesaid it was voated
to reserue a serteine track of land lyinge on the west side of

newlondon old road lyinge by the side of an alder swomp &
not to grant it to any person escept it be to the owners of the
saw mill: from this time untill the last of march next:—At
the meeting mentioned on the other side it was granted unto
Richard Carrier to take up his first Deuision of upland of
sixty akers * * * further granted unto John Clothyer ten
akers of land * * * further John skiner was Chosen to lay
out lands for this yeare—further granted unto Joseph dewey
his first diuision of upland * * * At the Meeting aforesaid
granted unto thomas brown aboute one aker of land at the
reare of his home lot on the south side of the governers brook:
further [granted unto samull Northam about ten acers of
upland on each side of a spreng of meadow at the long
meadow * * *

At a towne meeting held in Colchester Jenewary 11th:
1705-6 the acoumt which Joseph pumery gaue in of townes
debt & Credebt for euery perticqler man was exsepted erours
ondly exsepted—at the meetinge aforesaid it was granted to
euen Jones the liberty to take up thirty akers of upland on the
south side of the sixty akers which John addamss sold to mr
bulkley—at the meetinge aforesaid the towne remitted the for-
fitture of Moses rowlees lott: At the meeting aforesaid ebenezer Dibell & William roberd ware Chosen howards: : or to
impownd all hogs which are not ringed & yoaked—the town
voated to make a rate to defray the town charges—at the meetinge aforesaid the town voated to grant unto the owners of the
saw mill that thay should haue the two hundred pownd right
which was Condistionally granted the 3d Day of September
last—further at the same meeting ebenezer Dibell was Chosen
Constabell for this yeare—

At a Town meetinge held in Colchester Jenewary the 24th:
1705 it was voated to sequester all the lands at the west end
of the home lotts that are on the west side of the street betwene the said home lots & the first deuision of vplands: we

say we do sequester it to be & remain to be Town Commons for euer all former grants ondly exsepted: further at the same meetinge the town did also sequester all the lands suthward from Clemenc kithophels home lott To the Gourners brook & so down to the long meadow: to samull Gilberts first deuision & so to go along by the froont of those teer of lots northwardly untill it Com to a path Called browns path & so by that path unto the said Cithophels lot againe—further granted unto Joshua wheeler to make up what he wants in his home lott to be equall with other men in upland two akers for one—further what he wants in Meadow by the same Rule—

At the Meetinge Mentioned on the other side the towne granted unto Joseph wright thirty akers of land eastward if it be to be found which is to be part of his hundred aker Deuision: which is granted on Condistion that he bringe his brother Jonathan to Com & settell in this towne: At the Meetinge aforesd the towne granted unto John Chapman one hundred pownd lottment & fowr pounds in Mony on Condistion that he said chapman giue up to the town his Dwellinge hows in Colchester which stands on his home lott that Joyns to Nathaniell kaloggs lott south | To giue it vp to the towne at or before the first of may next—the town voated that said hows shall be Drawn to the place that the Town agreeth on: on the hill neere mr bulkeys—at the meetinge aforesaid the town granted unto euen Jones fiuety Akers of land to be taken up on the southwest side of mr bulkleys 1t Deuision: he relinquishing his former grants=at the meeting aforesaid it was voated that those persons that payd fiue pownds to the hundred pownd lotment at their first enteranc: shall now be abated the one half of thair towne rate that was published this Day prouided thay pay the other half quiatly.

At a Towne meetinge held in Colchester March the 20th: 1705-6 The Town voated to beuld a meeting hows of forty foots square prouided that thare be mony giuen enouf to procure the nailes & Glass—further the towne chose a Committie to Carie on the beuldinge the sd hows namely Serget Rowlee Decon skiner Johon Skiner Joseph chamberlin Thomas Browne —further the town voated to be at the charge with our Neighbour Townes to hire the County surveyr to run the bounds betwene us & them : at the meeting aforesd it was Granted unto the owners of the Sawmill libertie to take up fiuety akers of land at the place mentioned to be reserued for them at a town meeting Decembr 30 1705.

A towne meting held in Colchester Decembr 31: 1712 Micaiell Taintor was Chosen town Clerk—Select men chosen ware Capt Gilbert Left Wiat & mr Daniell Clark—Constables —Nathaniell foot & John hopson—lesters, ware John biglo Noah Wels & Jonathan Gillet — inspecters Joseph pumery & Joseph chamberlin—grand Jurymen, Samuell Northam & Joseph pumery—Colecterers to Gather the minesters Rate ware william Roberds Junr & Medad pumery & Josiah Gates—way wardens thomas Day senr Nathaniell Lomis & benjemin fox & benjamin Graues & moses Rowlee—fenc vewers Richard church & Jonathan Northam—Sealers of Leather chosen ware Decon Lomis & thomas Day—Noah Weles was chosen brander—at the meeting aforesaid the towne voated & granted to the reuerent mr bulkley for his salery for this yeare insuing sixty pownds as mony—further the town voted to add eight pownds to mr bulkleys salery for the year now past which sd eight pownds is to pay for his fire wood for the year Insewing : further ensine Skiner Nathaniell kellogg & Sergt ebenezer dible ware chosen to lay out Conuenient highwaise.

Jeneawary the 15th 1710 : 11=was a legall town meeting held in Colchester—the town voated to grant to Joseph prat to chang or throw up part of his Deuision on the hill viz : that as lyeth beyond the gutter Called stony guter & to take up so much at the east end of his deuision : further the town chose left

Wells Samull Northam Samull Lomis John Skiner & Decon
skiner to lay out high wais Whare thay are wanting in all
parts of the town as also to inspect those that are already layd
that thay may not be intruded into & make return to the town
—further voated & granted to the present owners of the saw
mill the Streame that Joseph pumery turned to sd Sawmill So
long as the sd owners maintain sd mill—further at the same
meeting was granted to charels williams John skiner Jonathan
Northam Nathaniell foot Liberty to set up a saw mill on pine
swamp brook & also liberty of half an acre on each side of the
sd brook to lay lodgs (logs, c. m. t.) & also liberty to take in
2 or thre acrs for a pasture & liberty of damme & to bueld sd
mill within one year & half from this Date & to haue the use
of the streame & land no longer then thay keep a saw mill
thare : but the land & stream to remain to the town—further
granted to Joseph pepone about fiue & twenty Rods of land for
to beueld upon : further at the same meeting granted unto Daniell Clark senr one hundred Acrs of land to take up the same
out & Clear from any and all the land that is sequestered for
town Comons : & also to defend it on his own charg from any
person or persons that may or shall lay claim thereunto :
whearas Richard church hath taken up thre acres of Comons
Joyning to that land which he bought of Samll Northam : the
town granted sd church sd thre acres of land on condistion that
he sd church throw up thre acrs out of his home lot to the Comons
in lew of it—further granted to Samul Spencer half an acre of
land neare his hows for a gardin plot to be taken up out of the
high way about fiue or six Rods from his hows betwene two
ledges of Rocks.

at the meting mentioned on the other side the town Considering that Capt John prentice hath bought seauenty acres of
land of John arnall & part of it is out of Stubineses claime or
bounds the town now grant to sd prentice that if the line betwixt hadam & Colchester tak in sd seauenty acres of land to

hadam bounds that so much of it as is out of stebenses bounds
or Comprehended in sd stebenses deed sd prentice shall haue
liberty to take up in another place.

March 3d 1703 layd out for Andrew Carrier his first deuision of upland lyinge on the north side of the mill Brook. * *

Nouember 6th : 1703 layd out for Andrew Carrier a home
lott Lyinge on ye south side of Joseph pumerys shepiantups
lott.

December 28th : 1708. at a legall Town meeting held in
Colchester Micaiell Tantor was Chosen town Clerk—Select
men Chosen ware Joseph Wright Nathaniell Lomis Micaiell
Taintor Sen—Joseph Dewey was chosen Constabell—Thomas
brown & ebenezer Skiner ware chosen Colecterers to gather
the Minesters & town Rates this yeare : listers Chosen ware
Joseph prat Nathaniell foot Micaiell Taintor Junr—listers
sworn aprell 2d 1709—Way wardens Chosen ware leftent
Weles Josiah strong ebenezer Coleman—fenc vewers, Chosen
ware John Adames Jvr Clemenc kithophell Noah Coleman &
benjamin Skiner—Daniell Clark was chosen pownd-keeper—
further voated to grant ye Reuerant mr Bulkley for his salery
this yeare fiuety pownds in prouision as mony : : further voated
that from this time the setting up a paper wherein is signified
the time when ye Select Men apoynt a town Meeting we say
that the seting up sd paper of notice on the meeting hows ten
days before such meeting shall be acounted sufiscient notice—
at the foresaid meeting the town voated to set the New meeting howss at one of the two places hearafter mentioned viz :
the one on the hill by the old one the other ond near the Corner of mr Rights lot that was James taylers—further at the
same meeting voated to levey a rate of one pownd & half of
flax or ninepenc in mony to one hvndred pownd Right & so
proportionably to be payd at or before the last of Jenewwary
next : to be paid to ye present Colecterers for the use of the
Comittie chosen to defend the towne in a cours of law which is

already cominced in sundry actions: further at the same Meeting it was voated that swine to run at large without rings &
yoaks for the year insueing—further voated to hire Thomas
brown to keep schoole two or thre Moonth: & to pay him
twenty & fowr shillings pr Moonth as mony to be payd the one
half out of the Country Rate & the other half to be payd by
the parenc of the Scholers.

At a legall town meeting held in Colchester Jenewary ye
14th: 1708–9 it was voated that the bownds betwixt lime &
Colchester shall be & is now exsepted to be acording to the line
Run by mr John plumb: further voated that ondly fowr akers
shall be acounted home lot land & that is now stated both for
the town plat & for the farmers that haue buelt or shall hearafter beuld out of the town—further at the same meeting
voated & exsepted of the line Run by Capt prentice august
26th: 1708 betwixt Newlondon & Colchester & that it shall be
recorded—further at the meeting aforesaid the town voated to
set the New meeting hows near the Corner of mr Rights lot
which he bought of James tayler.

at a legall town meeting held in Colchester febrewary the
26th: 1710=11 the town Considering of the grant made to
Joseph Dewey in Nouembr the 4th: 1706 of a lotment Called
one hundred pownd Right which was Condistionally granted
that is to say to beuld a fulling mill & also to settell an inhabitant on said lot &c & sd Dewey hath not performed the sd Condistions the town now do Release or remit unto said Joseph
Dewey the former Condistions of sd grant prouided that sd
Dewey Do pay to the town ten pownds in Currant mony besides the ten pownds which he hath formerly payd or was to
pay he giueing bill to the select men in behalf of the towne to
pay eight pownds of sd ten at or before the 10th of may next
from this Date & forty shillings within one year from this Date
& further to giue bond to the select men to the sum of twenty
pownds to repaier said fulling mill betwene this & the first of

may next & to keepe sd mill in good repaire fiue yeare next insuing may next aforesaid: & also to full cloth well workman like & as cheap as any other mill in the Colony—Joseph Dewey hath cleared the aboue obligation.

at a legall town Meeting held in Colchester October the 1t: 1711—the town Considering the great nesessety of a schole haue Chosen a Comitie to manage that afaire to finish the frame of a howse that Capt gilbert hath set up which stands neare the meeting hows: Capt gilbert haueing giuen the sd frame to the town: with the stones that are thare reseruing the chamber to himself which he the sd Capt Gilbert is to finish on his own charg: also sd gilbert shall haue Liberty to make use of said hows on sabath days: Capt Gilbert John Chapman sener Nathaniell Lomis Nathaniell kellogg ware chosen for the Comitie to manage the afaire abouesd & also to hire a schoolmaster as spedy as thay Can Conueniently for this winter—at the meeting abouesaid the town granted unto William Roberds Junr twenty & one acres of Land as it Lyeth Joyninge to the land which he sd Roberts bought of Joseph Dewey on the south & Comon or undeuided Land North west on the high way: east to run one hundred & sixty rods he the said Roberds paying twelue pownds in mony to the townsmen for the use of the town—at the meeting aforesaid the town granted unto Nathaniell foot the improuemt of the town hoome lot that lyeth Joyning to Josiah foots home lot so long as thay do not se cause to improue it other waise—further the town Chose Sergt prat & Nathaniell kellog to lay out a high way for a Country way or Rhoad from the north end of the town unto Jeremiahs reuer & make return to the towne.

Artecles of Agrement Betwen John Stubins & Daniell Stubins & Charles hill & Samul waler & Joshua hemsted & Joshua wheler as Comoners in a tract of Land in the Township of Colchester as thay alegg: the one partie & the Comittie for Colchester wth The Inhabetants of ye same Colchester the other partie which is as followeth (viz) 1rst all yt tract of land yt ye abouesd partie (viz) John Stubins Daniell Stubins Joshua hemsted Samuel waler & Joshua wheler: Do hearby guie & throw up all ye Right & title yt thay haue in ye abouesd tract of Land yt is to say all & euery part of all the land thay the abouesaid persons (viz) the aforenamed partie hath a good Right & a lawfull title unto, in Consideration of which the Comittie Abouesd for Colchester with the Inhabetants Doth agree yt ye sd· partie shall haue such a Nomber of home lots acording to thair proportion : of land within ye Township Containing By Estemation about ye quantetie of Eight Miles Square. yt is eight Mile euery way & also an equall proportion acording to the Nomber of home lots In the whole township: which shall Be deuided acording to Such Rules already Agreed upon. & such as thall Be agreed upon.   Thay Now faling in with vs for the promoting of the town : & Carieing on town afairs & thay are to be freed from Purchasing any other Land within ye township of Colchester exsepting yt tract of Land thay haue a good & lawfull title unto: & ye one half of thair home lots With the other Deuisions wch shall be aloted to them shall be free from charges (viz) town charges for seauen years from this Date: untill such time as thay shall sell all or a part or setell Inhabetants on sd Land: & the other half forthwith To Be setled & bare & pay equall proportion of town charges with the Rest . of the Inhabetants . which Charges shall Be Raised or leuyed as thay shall Put Inhabetants there . yt is to say for that part or half whare there is Liberty for the seauen years abouesaid: & we the abouesd partics haue Agreed as abouesd as witnes our hands this 21t Day of Nouembr: ano: Dom—one thousand Seauen hundred & one—In the presents of these Witncses Jonathan hill Shubaiell Rowlee— (Signed)

John Stubins Daniell Stubins d his Mark Charles hill Samuell Waller Joshua hemsted Joshua Wheler—

John Eliot Samuell Northam Nathaniell foot Micaiell Taintor Comittie for Colchester.

To All Christian people to whome these presents shall Com:
Micaiell Taintor John Skiner and John Bulkley send greeting:
whearas ye proprieters of ye town of Colchester in ye county
of hartford in ye colony of Conetecut Did at a meeting october
the 23d: 1717 : voate & agree to Releas unto ye Reuerand mr
peter thacher of milton in ye County of sufolk in ye prouinc of the
masachusets bay in N: england : all thair Right title & Intrest
in & to a certain tract of Land : included in his Claime within
the said township of Colchester obtained by a deed from capt
mason : & whearas ye sd proprietors Did at ye meeting aforesd
chuse & apoynt us ye abouementioned Micaiell Taintor John
skiner & John bulkey in thair name & behalf to giue a deed of
Releas of sd Land unto the sd peter thacher therefore know ye
yt we the said Micaiell Taintor Jno skiner & John bulkley for
& in Consideration of ye sum of twenty & fiue ponnds in hand
well & truly paid before the ensealing & Deliuery of these
presents : ye Receipt wherof to full satisfaction we do hearby
acknoleg haue giuen granted bargained sold aliened Remited &
released quited claime & confirmed & by these presents Do
fully freely clearly & absolutely giue grant bargain sell alien
enfeoff Remise Release quit claim & confirm unto ye said mr
peter thacher in his full quiat & peacable posestion & siezuer
now being & to his heirs and asigns for euer all ye estate Right
title Intrest share posestion proportion Inheretance property
Reuertion Remainder claim & demand wt soeuer : which we ye
sd Micaiell Taintor Jno bulkley & Jno skiner & ye proprioters
of ye township of Colchester euer had now haue or wch we or
thay or our or thair heigrs & asines in time to Com: can may
might should or in any wise ought to haue or claim of in & to
ye tract of Land abouesaid which is butted & bounded as followeth (viz) begining at a mapell tree near the pond & runing
from thenc westerly to a white oak tre standing about twenty
Rods southerly of n: london old Rhoad: & from thenc Runing
northeasterly to labanon line & from thenc Runing to norwich

southwest line & from thenc to the mapele tre aforesd. with all
ye preueleges Comoditise hereditements emoloments & apurtenances wtsouer thareof or thareunto belonging to haue & to
hold All & singuler ye aboue granted & Released premeses
with ye appurtenances & euery part & parcell thareof unto ye
sd mr peter thacher & to his heigrs & asigns for euer to his &
thair own sole & proper benefit & Behouf from hencforth & for
euer more peacably & quiatly without any maner of Reclaim
chaling contradiction of us Micaiell Taintor John skiner John
bulkley or any of ye proprioters of Colchester aforesaid our &
thair heirs or asigns & without any acoumlt Reckoning or areer
tharefor : to be guien Rendered or Don in time to Com to us
or them so yt neighther we the sd Micaiell Taintor Jno skiner
Jno bulkley nor any of ye proprioters of Colchester aforesd our
or thair heirs or asigns or any other person or persons : for us
or them or in our names Right or stead shall or will by any
wais or means hearafter haue, claim, chaling, demand any estat
Right title Intrest of in & to ye premeses or any part or parcell
tharof but of & from all euery action of Right estate Right title
Intrest claim & Demand of in & to ye premeses & euery part
& parcell tharof we & thay & euery of ym shall be uterly ex-
cluded & Debared by these presents : in witnes wharof we haue
set hearunto our hands & seals this twenty-third day of october
one thousand seauen hundred & seauenteen :

Wheras ms Elizabeth willson of hartford, Claiming Vnder
ebenezer Colman : who is one of the proprioters abouementioned : hath a certain tract of Land Included Within the
abouementioned Release : Containing about eighty acres : &
she Not haueing thrown up the same : It is to be understood
that we ye aboue mentioned Micaiell Taintor John skiner &
Jno bulkley Do exsept ye sd grant & Do not by these Prisents
Releas ye same to ye aboue mentioned mr thacher :

MICAIELL TAINTOR.
JOHN BULKLEY.
JOHN SKINER.

Memorandum yt on ye 7th Day of Janewary : 1717=18 :
Micaiell Taintor within named personally apeared before me
ye subscriber one of his Majests Justices of ye peace for the
County of hartford & frely acknoleged ye within Instrumt to
be his volentary act & Deed :

JOSHUA RIPLEY.

mr Jno Bulkley & Jno: Skiner within Named personally
appeared in Colchester ye day & year within written & acknoleged the within written Instrument to be thair fre & volentary
act & Deed Before me   MICAIELL TAINTOR,

Justice of peace.
Recorded Janey : 7th 1717=18.

" To All Christian Peopell to whome these shall Com Greeting   Whearas the inhabetants of the town of Colechester In the
Countie of Newlondon in her Majesties Colonie of Conetecot
In Newengland in America haveing formerly invited ye rev-
rant Mr John Bulkley Junr to Com settell & labor in ye work
of ye Minestry of the Gospell among them & for his Incoragement so to do haueing layd out & exspended a Considera-
bell Charg towards The beulding an hows for him on his own
land in the sd town : That is to say ye frameing raising & Cou-
ering the hows Makeing a Seller under it & beulding the chim-
nies &c : & ye sd John bulkley hath Acordingly Com & settled
& now for ye space of som years past Labored in the work of
the ministry of ye gospell as aforesd among them : In Consideration hearof the inhabetants of the sd town haue on ye 26th
Day of June last past unanemusly agreed & pased an act
whearby thay haue frely Giuen ye whole exspence & charg
laid out by them on ye sd hows to ye sd John bulkely & to his
heirgrs & Asignes for euer & also haue Nomenated & apoynted
& Authorize vs Joseph chamberlin shubaiell Rowlee & John
skiner inhabetants & for the present year select Men for the
sd town in thair name & behalf to make a deed for ye Confirmation of ye sd gift to ye sd John bulkley as by ye regester of

ye town May More fully Apear—Now know ye yt we ye sd
Joseph Chamberlin shubaiell Rowlee & John skiner inhabetants & for this present Select men of the town Aforesaid haue
Acording to ye trust reposed in us & Authoritie giuen to us as
aforesd in ye name & behalf of all ye inhabetants of the town
aforesaid & for them thair heigrs executors & administrators &
sucksesors frely Giuen Granted & pased ouer & do by these
presence frely Giue grant & pass ouer all ye exspence & Charg
laid out by them & euery of them upon the hows aforesaid &
the hows thereby so far erected & Acomplished : unto ye sd
John bulkly & to his heigrs & asigns for euer to haue & to hold
the same to him ye sd John bulkley & to his heigrs & Asignes
to his & thair own propper use & behoof for euer & for ye full
Confirmation hearof we ye Aboue Named select men do by
these presence Covinent & promice to & with ye sd John bulkley that we haue Good Right & lawfull Athoritie in & for ye
premeses & yt therefore he ye sd John bulkley & his heigrs &
asigns shall haue & hold the sd hows to him them & euery of
them & to his & thair own proper use & behoof from ye day
of ye Date hearof foreuer without any claime demand or other
molestation or disturbance of or from any of ye inhabetants of
ye Town aforesd or of or from any of them thair heigrs executors or administrators or sucksesors or any other person or
persons claiming by from or under them or any of them on ye
acounbt of ye premeses or any part or parsell thareof for euer
& all & euery ye inhabetentc Aforesd & thair heigrs executors
administrators Asignes & sucksesors shall & will at all times
allow warrant & defend the same—In testimony whareof we
haue set to our names & affixed our seals in Colechester aforesd
on ye 28 of october : anno Domi 1706.

SHUBIAELL ROWLEE
JOSEPH CHAMBERLIN.
JOHN SKINER.

Witnes JONATHAN GILLET.

6*

The Aboue Named Shubaiell Rowlee Joseph chamberlin &
John Skiner personally Appeared this 28th of octobr 1706 &
acknoliged the aboue written instrument To be thair own fre
& volentary act & deed Before Me

MICAIELL TAINTOR

her Majesties Justice of ye peace for Colechester.

" To all Christian peopell to whome these shall Com greeting know yee that I william shipman of Colechester in the
Colonie of Conettecott in newengland in Consideration of the
sum of fiueteene pownds in mony to me already secured as also
for Diuers other good Causes mouinge Me thereunto haue bargained sold alleinated & do by These presenc Make ouer. unto
timothy phelps son of Capt Timothy phelps of windsor in the
County of hartford in the Colonie Aforesaid : one thousand
acor right in a sertain track or parsell of land which was Giuen
by the Indian Called Joshua unto sundry persons in the town
of saybrook & Confirmed by the generall Court unto those
persons : & those legatees in Joshuas will of saybrook aforesaid haueing proseded in laying out som of those lands in order
to settell a towne there : I the aforesaid william shipman haueing a thre thousand acer right in the aforesaid lands haue thre
home lots layd out to me thare : one of the said home lots as
it lieth on the east side of the street of the Town plot & is in
bredth forty & thre rods : the length & whose land it Joyns to
on the sides May be more perticqlerly seene in the Map or
draught of the proseedings of the legatees aforesaid I the
Aforesaid William Shipman haue sold unto timothy phelps
aforesaid as also one thousand acer right belonging to said home
lott—furthermore I the said william shipman do Asert my
Right & titell & intrest in the land aforesaid & do hearby
Confirm unto timothy phelps aforesaid his heigrs executors
Adminestrators or asigns the home lott of forty & thre rods
wide & lying on the east side of the street as aforesaid : & the
one thousand Acer right aforesaid — & I do Athorise the

Aforesaid timothy phelps his heigrs or Asigns to take posestion of the homelott Aforesaid : & also to take all other deuisions of land belonging to A thousand Acer Right as they shall fall & I do inuest him or them with all the preueliges & Apurtenances belonging to a thousand acer right as much as I myself Could haue : & to act in all Matters in deuiding of lands & in settelment of the plantation as I Could do in a thousand Acer right—furthermore I the Aforesaid william shipman do bind My self My heigrs exseckotors Adminestrators to secure unto timothy phelps his heigrs exseckotors Adminestrators or Asigns the thousand acer right Aforesaid from any other gift grant Morgage dowrie thirds or any incumberanc of law whatsoeuer for the Confirmation of the premeses I the aforesaid William Shipman do sett to my hand & seal this tenth day of Aprell one thousand seauen hundred & fiue.

Signed sealed in the presenc of us Micaiell Taintor Thomas Inghamk.

his

WILLIAM W SHIPMAN.

Mark

William Shipman personally appeared this tenth day of Aprell one thousand seauen hundred & fiue & acknoliged the aboue written Instrument To be his own volentary act & deed before Me ·

MICAIELL TAINTOR Justice of Peace."

" 1701 Samuell Lomis hath granted a home Lott & Layd out in bredth 21 rods: in Length one hundred & sixty rods: bounded south on John Skiners home lott west & North on highwais east on the Comons—further Granted to Samuell Loomis meadow swomp & upland in the lew of meadow seauenteene akeres bounded north on Joseph pumeries land east on the Commons south on land of shubaiell Rowlees west on the lots in stebins his meadow also sixty akers of vpland Called first devision land laid out on the hill Called Carriers hill bounded north on Land of John Skiners south on land of John Addams senr east & west on the Commons "—

" May 1702 granted & layd out unto Thomas Skiner a home lot in length one hundred & sixty Rods in bredth 21 rods bounded east by the street North by John waters his home lot west on the Comons—further thomas skiner hath granted & layd out for his first Deuision sixty Akers Joyning to Micaiell Tantors land on the southeast side on the east side of the littell Meadow bounded 1t by a run of water by Micaiell Taintors land so runeth westerly by sd tantor & the high way one hundred & thirty & eight Rods to bounds set by the highway * *

To all people to whome these presenc shall Com Joseph Chamberlin of the Towne of Colechester in the Countie of hartford in har Majesties Colonie of Conettecot in New england sendeth greeting know ye that the sd Joseph Chamberlin for & in Consideration of the sum of nineteen pownds Currant Mony well & truly payd or legally secuerd to be payd from samuell dickerson of the town of hadley in the Countie of hamshier in har Majesties prouince of the Masachusets in Newengland aforsd * * * * & lastly that he the said Joseph Chamberlin & his heigrs shall & will at the reasonabel request & at the propper Cost & Charges in the law of him the said Samuell dickerson his heigrs & assignes from time to time make due perform or execute or Cause to be made don performed & executed all & euery such further grants acts & assuerences in the law for the further better & more perfect insuering & suer makeing of the sd before bargained land & premeses unto the said Samuell dickerson his heigrs & assigns for euer acording to the true intent & Meaning of these presence as by the sd Samuell Dickerson his heigrs or asignes or his or thair Counsell larned in the law shall reasonabelly be deuised aduised & requiered in testimony whareof the sd Joseph Chamberlin hath hearunto set to his hand & seal this ninth

day of aprell in the eighth year of the Reign of our souerran
Lady ann : of england Scotland franc & Ierland Queen &c—
Anoqua Domini 1709.   JOSEPH CHAMBERLIN

Signed sealed in the presence of vs witneses John Day Joseph pratt.

Colchester aprell the ninth in the eighth year of har Maijes-
ties reigne Anaqua Domini 1709 the aboue named Joseph
Chamberlin personally appeared before me the subscriber har
Majesties Justic of the peac for the County of hartford & ack-
noliged the aboue written instrument to be his volentary act &
Deed.   MICAIELL TAINTOR Justice peac."

To All Christian People to whome these presents Shall Com
greeting know yee that I Micaiell Taintor of the towne of
Colchester in the County of hartford within her Majests Colony of Conettecot in Newengland in Consideration of thirty &
fiue pownds Curent mony to me well & truly paid by Ms abigaiel Lord Widow of the town of hartford of the County &
Colony aforesd tharwith I do acknolig my self fully Satisfied
& Contented & by these presents Do exonerate acquitt & dis-
charge ye Sd abigaill Lord her heigrs executors, adminestrs for
euer by these presents I ye sd Micaiell Taintor with ye fre
Consent of my wife mabell Taintor haue giuen granted bargained Sold aliened Conueyed & Confirmed & by these presents Do fully frely & absolutely giue Grant bargain Sell
Conuey & Confirm unto her heigrs & assines foreuer one tract
of Land Situat Lying & being in ye township of Colchester
aforesd & south easterly of a pond Called the Long pond which
said Land is Called my third Dcuision & is laid out on ye west
side of Lime Rhoad bounded as followeth : (viz) north by land
of Joshua Whelers South with land Layd out to Isreal Wiat
Now belonging to ye said abigaill Lord easterly with undeuided Land west With ye Brook that Coms out of ye aforesaid
pond the length east & west is one hundred & sixty Rods the

bredth north & south is one hundred Rods being in estemation
one hundred acres be ye same more or Less to haue & to hold
the said granted premises preueliges Comodities to ye same
belonging or any waise appertaining to her the said abigaill
Lord her heigrs executors adminestratrs & assignes for euer to
her & their own proper benefit use & behouf for cuer & I ye
sd Micaiell Taintor for me my heigrs executors adminestratrs
Do Couenant promice & grant to & with ye sd abigaiell Lord
her heigrs & assines yt before & at ye time of ye ensealing &
deliuery of these presents I am ye tru sole & lawfull owner
of ye aboue bargained premeses & am Lawfully siezed & pos-
essed of ye same in mine own proper Right as a good perfect
& absolute estate of inheritance in fee simple & haue in my
self good right full power & Lawfull athority to sell Conuey &
Confirm sd granted & bargined premeses in maner as abouesd
& yt ye sd abigaill Lord her heigrs & assines shall & may from
time to time & at all times for euer herafter by force & vertue
of thes presents Lawfuly peacably & quiatly haue hold use
ocupie posess & injoy ye sd Demized & Bargained premeses
fre & Clear & frely & Clearly acquited & discharged of & from
all & all maner of former & other gifts grants bargains Sales
Leases Mortgages Wills Inteiles Joynters Dowries Judgments
executions Incomberences furthermore I ye Sd Micaiell Taintor for my self my heigrs executors adminestratrs Do Couenant & ingage the sd Demized & bargined premeses to her ye
sd abigail Lord her heigrs & assines against ye Lawfull Claims
& demands of any person or persons wtsoeuer for euer hearafter to warrant Secuer & defend to all intents & purposes of
Law wtsoeuer In witnes hearof I ye said Micaiell Taintor
haue hearunto set to my hand & seal this twenty & sixth Day
of May in tweluth year of her majests Reign Anoqua Domini: 1713—   MICAIELL TAINTOR L. S.

Signed & Sealed in the presents of us Witneses Samuel
Smith Ebenezer Mead—entered on record the Date abouesaid.

May 26th: 1713 the aboue Named Micaiell Taintor Appeared personally in hartford & acknoliged the aboue written Instrument to be his fre & volentary act & Deed before me

SAMUEL SMITH Justice.

To All Christian people to whome these shall Com greeting know ye yt William Shipman of hebron in har majesties Colonie of Conettecot in Newengland: in & for the sum of fiueteen pownds in mony already secuered & I do declare that before the signing & sealing hearof I am tharewith fully satisfied & contented: from Jacob Root of Northhampton in the County of hamshier in the prouince of the masachustts in Newengland aforesd haue bargained giuen granted sold allicned Conueyed & Confirmed & by these do fully frely & absolutely giue grant bargin sell & Conuey & Confirm to him the sd Jacob Root & his heigrs & assignes for euer one thousand acre right in a tract of land which was giuen by the indian Called Joshua unto Sundry persons of ye town of saybrook which sd propriators haue proseeded to lay out homlots on sd land in order to the setling a town I ye sd william shipman haue sold one of sd home lots as it lyeth sittuat in ye east deuision of homelots being in length eighty rods: in bredth sixty & two rods bounding north on the homelot of Capt Samuell Jons south on mr thomas buckingham east on a high way & west on another tear of lots being in estemation thirty & one acres be it more or less all which home lot & euery part of it together with the thousand acre Right belonging to it I do bequeath make ouer & conuey & Confirm unto ye sd Jacob root * * * in witnes wharcof I the sd william shipman do set to my hand & seal this 24th day of Jenwary 1705.

his

WILLIAM M SHIPMAN.

mark

william shipman personally apeared the day & year abouesd

& acknoliged the aboue written instrument to be his fre act & deed before me MICA'LL TAINTOR Justice.

Signed sealed & deliuered in presence of thomas day James brown.

"To all people to whome these shall Com John Clother of Colchester within the Countie of hartford within her Majesties Colony of Conettecot husbandman sendeth greeting &c: know ye that I the sd John Clother for & in Consideration of the sum of seauenty & fiue pownds in mony to me in hand before the insealing hearof well & truly paid by thomas allien of killingley in the County of Newlondon in the abouesaid Colony in Newengland yeoman the receipt wharof I do hearby acknolig & myself tharewith fully satisfied & Contented & therof & euery part & parsell tharof do exonerate acquit & discharg the said thomas allien his heigrs executors adminestrators & assignes for euer by these presents haue Giuen granted bargained sold aliened enfeefed & Confirmed * * * unto the said thomas allien his haigrs & asigns one Mesuage containing one mantion howse with thirty & fiue acres by estemation be it more or less of upland swomp & Arrable ground sd premeses sittuat lying & being in Colchester * * * in witnes wharof I ye sd John Clother haue hearto set my hand & seall this twenty-first day of July in ye year of our lord one thousand seaun hundred & twelue & in ye tenth year of ye reine of our soueran Lady Ann of great brittain Queen defender of the faith

JOHN CLOTHER.

Signed sealed & deliured in presents of vs
James brown James taylor Isaac Rowlee.

July 25th: 1712 John Clother the Granter personally appeared in Colchester before me the subscriber her Majestics Justice of the peace for the County of hartford & acknoliged the aboue written Instrument to be his fre & vollentary act & Deed MICAIELL TAINTOR Justice peace.

Entered on Record July 25th: 1712."

" These Lines signifie that I ówanecoe sachem of Mohegan son of vncas Doe Confirme by these presenc vnto Danll Mason son of Major John Mason of Norwich a tract of Land lying on the east side of a pond by vs Called wongupsack near Land by my father vncas given unto Jeremiah adams of hartford this Land I say is by me Confirmed unto Danill Mason son of Major John Mason aboue mentioned to him the sd Danll Mason his heigrs & asignes from Me my heigrs & assignes for euer : that Neighther I nor any by My Means shall disturb or molest the sd Mason his heigrs or Asignes in the quiat posestion of sd Land as it was by my father uncas granted unto the sd Major John Mason & by him Giuen unto the sd Danll Mason : the boundaries are as followeth : from a Rock by the sd pond Running Northward twelue scoar Rods bounded west upon the pond unto a tre Marked toward the Northward end of sd pond extending eastward ten scoar Rods unto two Rocks Marked O M which are the Northeast & southeast bounds of sd Land with thirty acres of Meadow lying eastward of sd Land all which Land & Meadow I do hearby Confirm unto the sd Daniell Mason as aboue sd unto which I haue set my hand & seall this first day of october in the year sixteen hundred & ninetie & two : witnes my hand & seal :

the Mark of OANECO

witnes John Mason & John Mason son of Samull Mason.

oaneco Apeared & acknoliged the aboue writen instrument before me the date aboue Mentioned : Samull Mason asistnt.

entered on Record febey 25 : 1708–9—

" To All Christian People to whome these shall Com John More & Joshua More both of Newlondon in the Colony of Conetecot send Greeting know ye That for & in Consideration of the sum of fourteene pownds in Corent mony Receaued of & from Noah Weles of Lime in sd Colonie the receit wharof the sd John More & Joshua More Doth acknolig & thare-

upon acquite & discharg the sd Noah Welles his heigrs &
Asigns foreuer : haue Giuen granted bargined & sold alienated
enfefued & Confirmed & by these presenc ye sd John More &
Joshua More Do for them Selues thair heigrs executors & adminestrators Clearly & absolutely Giue grant Bargin sell enfefe
& Confirm unto the sd Noah Welles his heairs & Asignes for
euer a sertain tract & parsell of Land situate in the township
of Colechester in sd Colonie which is the full half of one-sixth
part of a tract of land Giuen by uncas Late sachem of Mohe-
gen to John & Daniell Stubins of New london & bounded as
by uncas his deed sheweth the which half of sd sixth part the
sd John & Joshua More hath by Deed from John & Daniell
Stubins aforesd bareing Date Jeneweary the sixtenth one thousand six hundred ninety eight nine & the sd John More &
Joshua More, doth promice Couenant Grant to & with the sd
Noah Welles his heigrs & Asignes that they are the true lawfull owner of the premeses at the time of the insealing hearof
& haue Good right full power to dispose of the same to ye sd
noah Welles his heigrs & Asignes for euer & the said Noah
Welles his heigrs & Asignes shall & may from time to time &
at all times hearafter foreuer peacabely & quiatly haue hold
use posess & injoy the aboue bargined premeses with all the
preueliges & apurtenences thereunto belonging to ye sole benefit & behoofe of ye said Noah Welles his heigrs & Asignes
for euer without Any lett hinderanc Molestation or objection
of them the sd John More Joshua More their heigrs executors
admin'tors or any person or persons whatsoeuer by means of
any of us—In witnes whareof The sd John & Joshua More
haue set to thair hands & seals this 5th Day of June 1706

JOHN MORE

JOSHUA MORE

signed sealed in the presenc of vs John hough Carye La-
tham

October 22d 1706—John More & Joshua More personally

appeared & acknoliged the aboue instrument to be thair act &
Deed Before me   DANIELL WITHERLE Asistant

entered on Record ye same Date abouesd " (by Micaiell
Taintor Recorder)

To All Christian people to whome these shall Com Greeting
Know Yee That I Joshua Fairbanks of the towne of Wren-
tum within her Majsts prouince of the Masachusets Bay in
New england in Consideration of a Vallewable Sum of Mony
to me well & truly paid by Robert Ransom of The towne of
Colchester in the County of hartford within her Majes'ts Colony
of Conetecot in New england aforesaid tharwith I do acknolig
My Self Satisfied Contented & paid By these presents haue
Giuen granted Bargined Sold Asined set ouer & Confirmed &
by these presents do for My self my heigrs executors & adminest'rs fully frely & absolutely Asigne set ouer & Confirm
unto the said Robert Ransom & to his heigrs & assigns for
euer all my Right title Intrest in & to ye Lands mentioned in
the Deed from Benjamin Skiner on the other side I say I do
fully frely Assine set ouer unto him the said Robert Ransom
his heigrs & assines the afores said Right & euery part thareof
as it is thare mentioned as much as I my self Could haue in
witnes hearof I the Said Joshua fairbanks haue set to my hand
& seal this third Day of Nouemb'r in the tweluth year of her
Majestis Reigne Ano : Domini : 1713—
                          JOSHUA FAIRBANKS
Signed Sealed & Delivered in the
   presents of Vs Witness   James Newton Micaiell Taintor

entered on Record the 4th : Nouembr : 1713

Nouemb ye 4th : 1713 : Joshua fairbanks the Granter appeared in Colchester before me the subscriber one of her Majesties Justices of the peace for the County of hartford &
acknoliged the aboue Written Instrument to be his fre & volentary act & Deed Micaiell Taintor Justice peace—

To All People to whome these shall Com Left James harris
of Colchester in ye County of hartford in his Majestis Colony
of Conettecut sends Greeting &c know ye yt I ye sd James
harris for diuers good Causes & Considerations me hearunto
moueing but more espestialy for & In Consideration of ye
erecting & beulding a meeting hows for ye publick worship of
god: within ye new parrish partly in Colchester, & partly in
ye township of Lyme: Comonly Called new salem: haue
giuen granted aliened enfeofed and Confirmed: & by these
presents do fully Clearly & absolutely giue grant alien enfeoff
Conuey & Confirm unto Left Jno holmes Sergt thomas Jones
& mr pelatiah bliss all of Colchester aforesd: as feffces in
trust: unto them thair heirs Executors & adm'tes &c=for
euer as fees in trust one Certain tract or parsell of Land:
Containing by Estemation two acers for ye uses hearafter mentioned & for no other use or end Sd Land lying & being in ye
township of Colchester aforesd; & within sd parrish; & is
butted & bounded as followeth (viz) begining at a white *oake*
tree: being ye sowwest Corner bounds: sd tre standing In ye
deuiding line betwixt Colchester & lyme: & markt on thre
sids form thenc Runing east in ye deuiding line to a walnut
tre markt with a heap of stones about it which is a bound
markt tre betwen Colchester & Lyme from thenc Runing Due
north by land of ye sd James harrises to a stake & heap of
stones: to Mr. bliss his land: then Runing westerly by sd blises
land to a stake & stones standing Due north from ye first mentioned white oake tree the abuesd tract of Land Lying west
about twelue or fifteen Rods from ye hows of James haris
Jun'r to haue & to hold ye sd giuen & granted premeses to
them their hiers executors & adminest'rs for euer to them ye
sd Jno holms thomas Jones & pelatiah bliss as ffees in trust; to
hold for the use of ye abouesd parrish for ye beulding of a
prisbeterian meeting hows, & for a buering place & for A train-
ing field: the abouesd meeting hows to be beult for the Inhabitants tharein to worship god in ye prisbeterian faith: fur-

thermore I ye sd James harris do for my self my heirs Executors & admins'trs Couen't promice & grant to & with ye sd
Jno holms thomas Jones & pelatiah bliss thair heirs Ex-
ecut'r & admines'te: yt before ye ensealing hearof I am ye true
Sole & lawfull owner of ye aboue giuen & granted premeses
& am Lawfully sizsed & posesed of ye same in mine own
proper Right as a good perfect & absolute estate of Inhere-
tants in fee simple: & haue in my self good right & lawfull
athorety to giue Grant & dispose of ye same in maner as
abouesd & yt thay ye said John holms thomas Jones & plata-
tiah bliss shall & may from time to time & at all times foreuer
hearafter peacably & quiatly haue hold use ocupie posess &
Injoy the aboue demised & granted premeses for ye usees &
ends abouementioned for euer hearafter fre & Clear from all
Incomberances whatsoeuer: & for euer to warrant & defend
the aboue giuen & granted premeses against ye lawfull Claims
& demands of any person or persons whomesoeuer: In witnes hearof I ye said James harris haue hearunto set my hand
& seal this tenth Day of Nouember in the thirteenth year of
his Majestis Reign George of great brittain King &c; & in ye
year of our lord god 1726:   JAMES HARRIS   (sel)

Signed sealed & deliuered In the
    presence of vs—   James Tredway Daniell Galusiah
Recorded december 12th: 1726—

Colchester Decemb'r ye 12th 1726—then Left James harris
the Granter & subscriber personally appeared before me the
underwrighter & acknoleged the aboue written Instrument to
be his free & vollentary act & deed—
                    Micaiell Taintor Justice of ye Peace

To All Christian People to whome these shall Com greeting
know ye yt I Micaiell Taintor of Colchester in ye County of
hartford within his Majestis Colony of Conettecut In New england: in & for ye Consideration of eighty pounds Curent
money to me in hand paid or secuered to be paid from Richard
        7*

Robins of wethr'field in the County & Colony aforesd tharewith I acknoleg myself fully satisfied & Contented & by these presents do exonerate & acquit ye sd Richard Robins his heirs executors & adminis'trs for euer by these presents haue giuen granted bargained sold aliened enfeoffed Conueyed & Confirmed & by these presents do fully frely & absolutely giue grant bargain sel Conuey & Confirm vnto him ye sd Richard Robins his heirs & assigns for euer, one hundred acers of land in the township of Colchester aforesd; & is my fifth deuision already Drawn for at a meeting of the proprieters: held october ye 12th: 1724 as apears of Record which acrued to me by vertue of a two hundred pound Right in ye township of sd Colchester ye which fifth Deuision is already Drawn for as abouesd: but not yet laid out: the which ye sd Richard Robins his heirs & asigns shall & may by vertue of these presents lay out & Record To him or themselues in ye undeuided land in Colchester the wch when it is orderly laid out,: it being in the Draught aforesd ye nomber of 53 yt then the sd Richard Robins his heirs & assigns shall haue & hold ye sd granted premeses preueleges comodetis to ye same belonging or in any wise apertaining to him ye said Richard Robins his heirs & assigns for euer * * * * * * In witness hearof I ye sd Micaiell Taintor haue set to my hand & seal this fifteenth Day of nouembr in the twelulth year of ye Reign of our Soueran lord George of Great brittain King &c & in ye year of our lord An: Dom: 1725—   Micaiell Taintor   (sel)

Signed Sealed & deliuered In
    the presence of   Joseph Wright Joseph Wright Junr
    Recorded ye same date abouesd—

Colchester March ye: 14th: 1726: I ye under wrighter (& grantor & subscriber to ye aboue written Instrument: Do: under my office: oath) acknoleg ye aboue written Instrument to be my fre & vollentary act & Deed—

                Micaiell taintor Justice of ye Peace

To All Christian People to whome these shall Com Greeting know yee yt I Micaiell Taintor of Colchester in ye County of hartford in his Majestis Colony of Conettecut in Newengland haueing formerly sold to ms Abigaiell Lord now Abigaiell woodbridg of hartford aforesaid: one hundred acers of Land in ye township of Colchester aforesd: as appears by a Deed bareing Date ye 26th Day of may 1713: but ye settlement of the bounds betwixt haddam & Colchester hath taken of from sd hundred acers with yt taken of from yt which Isreal wyat sold to ye sd abigail Lord twenty & one acers: therfore I hauc Caused a new suruey of ye said land with an alteration of Length & breadth of ye land yt is in ye same place as it was set forth in ye former Deed which is seauenty nine acers:) which is as followeth bounded east with Lyme Rhoad one hundred & fiue Rods * * * * * * * *   I do therefore in Consideration yt mr timothy woodbridg & abigaill woodbridg his wife Do giue up to me in way of exchang for this Deed ye former Deed bareing Date may 28th: 1713: that then ye said mr timothy woodbridg & abigail ₁woodbridg his wife: & her heirs & assigns shall Haue & hold ye sd hundred acers of Land acording to ye bounds & butments set forth in this Deed * * * * *   in witnes hearof I haue hearunto set my hand & seal ye thirty first Day of may An: Dom; 1720:   MICAIELL TAINTOR

Signed Sealed & deliuered
    In ye presence of   Dauid Goodrich Elisha Lord—

Recorded the same date abousd   .

May 31t 1720: then personally appeared before me ye subscriber: Mr Micaiell Taintor the granter & subscriber hearof & acknoleged the aboue written Instrument to be his fre act and Deed—Dauid Goodrich Justice of Peace

    To All Christian people to whom these shall Com greeting

know ye that I Joseph Dewey of Colchester in ye County of hartford & Colony of Conettecut in New england in Consideration of a grant of land to william Roberds Junr made By ye proprioters of Colchester which was ten acres as appears of Record in the Proprioters Book & also at the same time viz :— Sept : 30th : 1715 : granted to myself about seauen acres ; tharewith I acknolege myself fully satisfied & Contented & By these Presents Do acquit & Discharg the Said Proprioters & thair heigrs & Asigns forcuer : By these Presents haue giuen granted Bargained sold Alienated enfeoffed Conueyd & Confirmed & By these presents haue giuen granted Bargained sold Allienated Conueyed & Confirmed unto Micaiell Taintor who was appoynted by the aboue Said Proprioters to take a deed of me for one tract of Land Sittuate in the township of said Colchester & was the Rear of John Jonsons home lot : formerly Josiah strongs * * * * In witness hearof I the Sd Joseph Dewey haue set to my hand & seal this first Day of Decemb'r one thousand seauen hundred & fifteen—

JOSEPH DEWEY (seal)

Signed Sealed in ye Presents of vs

Thomas Aleson Sarah Taintor

This Deed Recorded the Same Date Abouc said

Joseph Dewey, ye Granter appeared In Colchester ye Day & year Aboue Written & acknoledged The aboue Written Instrument To Be his fre act & Deed Before me

Micaiell Taintor Justice of peace

" This Indentuer made ye twenty seauenth Day of october in the eleauenth year of the Reigne of our soueraign Lady ann By ye Grace of god of Great Brittain franc & Ierland Queen Defender of the faith &c Anaq: Domini one thousand seauen hundred & twelue Betwene Richard tozer of Colches-

ter in ye County of hartford in the Colony of Conettecot in
New england husbandman on ye one party & Gurdan saltonstall of New London : in the Colony aforesaid esqr of the
other partie witneseth that the said Richard tozer for & in Consideration of ye summ of twenty pownds Currant siluer mony
of New-england : to him in hand before the sineing & deliuery
of these presents well and truly paid by ye said Gurdon saltonstall esq. the receipt wharof to full Content & satisfaction
he ye said Richard tozer doth hearby acknolig & tharof & of
euery part & parcell tharof doth quit & discharg the said Gurdon saltonstall esqr. his heigrs executors adminestrators & assigns & euery of them for euer by these presents he the sd
Richard tozer hath giuen granted bargained & sold Alienated
enfeoffed Conueyed & Confirmed & by these presents doth
fully frely Clearly and absolutely giue Grant bargain sell alien
enfeoff Conuey & Confirm unto the sd Gurdon saltonstall esqr
his heigrs & asigns for euer the one twenty fowrth part of a
Certain tract of Land & meadow Lying in the township of
Colchester aforesaid : Exsepting thirty acres tharof (which
part of Land abouesaid was bought By the sd tozer of mr John
arnald of New-london & by sd arnald of mr Charles hill Late
of New-london deceased and by sd hill of John stebns Daniell
Stubns and Christopher Stubins the whole of which tract was
Giuen by uncas Chief Sachem of mohegan unto the stubnses
& bounded out to them by Poquiunk son of sd uncas to gether
with all the howsings buildings fences trees waters streams
Riuers profits preueliges emoluments heraditaments & apurtenances whatsoeuer unto the said Lands belonging or any waise
apertaining to the sd twenty fowrth part of the abouesd
whole tract * * * * prouided alwaise & vpon Condistion Neuertheless & it is ye true Intent & meaning of these
presents that if the abouenamed Richard tozer his heigrs executors or administrators or any of them shall & do well &
truly pay or Cause to be paid unto the aboue named Gurdon

saltonstall esqr his heigrs execu'ts admincstrators Certain attorney or assings the full & Just summ of twenty pownds Currant mony of New-england Abouesaid with Lawfull Intrest for the same on or before the twenty seauenth Day of october which will be in the year of our Lord one thousand Seauen hundred & fowrteen without any fraud or further delay: then this present Deed of bargain & sale or morgage & euery grant Clause & artecle therein Contained shall Cease determin be utterly void & of none efect or ele to be and remain of full force & vertue in witness wharof the partie aboue mentioned to these presents hath set to his hand & seal the day & yeare first aboue writen Richard tozer—N. london octob'r 27 : 1712 : then Receud of Gurdon *saltonston* Esqr the within mentioned summ of twenty pownds—I say recud by me Richard Tozer— Entered on Record March ye 5th 1713 : 14 :"—

Colchester December 3 1730 then Lef: Skiner ye subscriber personally appeared before me the under wrighter & acknoledged the foregoing Instrument to be his free act & Deed

Micaiell Taintor Justice of Peace

Signed Scaled & deliuered in ye presence of us

her
Micaiell Taintor Mabel M Taintor
mark

Edward fuller & elizabeth Rowlee ware maried July 21t : 1715 Ann was b. May 28th. 1716—Abigaiell b. Aprell ye 3d—1718—Sarah b. July ye 8th = 1719—Silence b. May 22d = 1721—febee b. aprell 18th = 1723—Unice b. May 12th = 1726—David b. Janewy 28th : 1728.

Mary Daughter to James Taylor b. Nouembr ye 9th : 1701 —Martha b. Nouembr 29th—1704 = James b. August ye 16th = 1707 Bethia b. Nouembr : 12th—1709 = Leuie (Levi, c. m. t)b. March 17 : 1713

Richard Skiner & hanah prat ware m. Nouembr : 24 : 1708 = hannah b. aprell ye 16—1714—

Nalhaniel foot & Ann Clark ware m. July ye 4th : 1711—
Nathaniell b. May 28th : 1712=Isreall b. October 16th=1713
=An b. August 26th : 1715—Daniell b. Feb. y : 6=1716=
17=Charles b. Decemb 16th=1718

Ebenezer Coleman & ruth Nieles ware married March 11th
1704=5 niels b. februy : 20th—1706=7 at fowr of the Clock
in the morning—Ruth b. June 20th : 1709 at 3 of the Clock
in the morning—Mahittabel b. July 14th—1713,, at 5 of the
clock in the morning—Mary b. appell ye 8th, 1718 about thre
of the clock in the afternoon—

thomas Gurstin and Sarah holms ware m. June ye 7th=
1722—thomas son of thomas Gurstin b. July 19th, 1725=

John hopson & Sarah Northam m. Janewary 1704=Mary
b. July 2 : 1705=John b. Nouembr : 12 : 1707—Sarah the
wife of John hopson Dyed march 16th : 1708=John hopson
& elizabeth Day m. June ye 6th : 1710—elizabeth b. may : the
1t : 1711—John hopson Dyed febrewary the 22d : 1714—

Joseph wright had a son born Janewary ye 17th : 1702 : &
Dyed Jenewary 28th : 1702—Joseph was b. octobr ye 15th :
4704 : at nine clock in the euening on saterday—Ann b. August ye 3d 1707 : on a Sabath Day in ye euening—Sarah b.
aprell ye 5th : 1710 on munday & Dyed August 17th : 1710
Timothy b. March ye 5th : 1712 : John b. Janey 2d : 1715 :
on a Sabath Day night—Dudley b. Aprell 6th : 1717 ; on a
Saterday morning between break of Day & Sun Riseing=
John Dyed October 25th : 1718=Mary b. Nouember ye 15th :
1719 : early in ye morning on ye sabath=John wright the 2d
son to Joseph wright b. Janewary ye 12th ; 1724-5—on Sabath Day night about ten of ye elock—

William Chamberlin & Sarah Day m. Jenewary the 4th :
1710=11—William b. Jenewary ye 22d : 1711-12=peleg b.
Nouemb: 28 : 1713—John b. Jenewary ye 10th : 1715—16—

Sarah daughter to John Skiner b. July 17 : 1697—An b.
Octobr ye 1t : 1700 John b. August ye 30th : 1703—Daniell

b. August 30th: 1705—Joanah b. Jenewary 27th: 1707—
Joseph b. October ye 7th: 1710—Aron b. June ye 14th:
1713—

Noah Weles & Sarah wyat ware Married Aprell ye 15th:
1714. Isreall Wyat son to Noah Weles & Sarah his wife
was b. Decemb: 17: 1714—Jerusha b. Janeway 6th: 1716:
17—Jerusha Dyed December 17th: 1717=noah b. Septembr,
25th: 1718—Sarah b. Jenewary ye 12th: 1720=21—Dauid
b. Septembr 10=1723—Moses b. october ye 3d.—1725—
Gidion b. Janewary 22d:—1728-9—James Brown & Anne
wickwire m. october ye 14th: 1714—James b. Septembr ye
7th: 1715—

Abigaiell Daughter to Jonathan Cutler b. August 28th:
1711—Jonathan b. August 17th: 1713—Beach son to Jonathan Cutler b. July 4th: 1716

James Newton & Susanah Wyat were m. may 31th: 1716
—Dorothy b. february 25th: 171$\frac{7}{8}$—John b. Sept 30th: 1719
—James b. June 27th: 1721—Isreall b. feby ye 17: 1725—
thomas b. August ye 4th: 1728—& Died ye 21 Day of Septembr following. Dinah b. febry 24: 1730.

Samuell Knight & Mary Ransom m. Nouembr. 29: 1716—
Joshua b. June 20th: 1721—Mary b. July 13th: 1724—
Lydia b. June 26th: 1730

Daniell Chapman & Retern Wintworth m. March 22d:
1713—paul b. aprell ye 12th: 1714—Retern b. Decemb:
23: 1715—Marthah b. July ye 2d: 1717—another Daughter
born aprell 1719: and was still born—Sarah b. June ye 1t:
1720—Daniell b. Aprell ye 10th: 1722—Silas b. aprell ye
18th: 1724—Elias b. Janewary ye 14th: 172$\frac{5}{8}$—barnabus b.
ye 28th Day of March 1728

Sarah Daugter to thomas addams b. februwary ye 1t: 171$\frac{4}{}$
—Abigaiell b. March ye 3d: 171$\frac{7}{8}$—Thomas b. August ye
30th: 1719—Elizabeth b. Nouembr 3d: 1720—hannah b.
July 4th: 1722—Elijah b. may ye 30th: 1724—Mary &

Marthah twins b. March ye 17th : 1727—Lydia b. July 16th : 1729—(The next & last birth in the hand of Col Bulkley, viz.) " Elisha b. Septr 28th 1732"—

Benjamin addams & Mary Lomis m. Nouembr ye 25th= 1719—Benjamin b. Aprell ye 8th=1721—

Joseph pumery & Sarra beebe ware m. August 2d : 1727— Sarah the wife of Joseph pumery Dyed Septembr 3d :— 1728—

John nox & Elizabeth Roberds m. Aprell ye 20th : 1720— Elizabeth b. March 28th—1726—

mr Judah Lewes & Sarah Kellogg m. feby 19th—1728-9

february 15th : 1715=16 John whitcom & mahitable Dun- han m.—Jemima b. february 24th : 1716=17—John b. Jane- wary ye 13th : 1718=19—mahitable b. aprell ye 9th—1722— Job b. may ye 8th : 1724—mary b. Septr ye 15th : 1726— Isaac b. august 24th : 1728—(The next birth recorded by Col. Bulkley, viz.) Israell b. March 13th : 1733—

Noah pumory & Elizabeth Sterling m. Decembr : 16 : 1724 —Noah b. october ye 8th : 1725—Daniell b. october 13th— 1727—

Seth Dean & Ann Skiner m. october 29th : 1721—Aaron Gillet & hanah Clark m. July 10th : 1728—

John Brown & marah Chandler m. March ye 20th : 1710— Elizabeth b. Decembr 20th—1710—John b. Aprell ye 4th : 1715—hannah b. June 26th : 1717—Sarah b. Janewary ye 6th : 1719—20—timothy b. Decemb ye 3d : 1721—Nehe- miah b. September ye 26th : 1726—Jedediah b. March 21 : 1729

Joseph foot & Ann Clother m. Decembr 12th : 1719—am- bross b. Aprell ye 3d—1723—Jeremiah b. october ye 11th : 1725—

Jonathan Kellogg & ann Newton m. ye 3d Day of Jane- wary 1710—11—Jonathan b. Septemb ye 18th : 1712—Jo- seph b. June ye 6th : 1714—Margeree b. augst : ye 10 :

1716—(the three next births in the hand of Col. Bulkley, viz.) Stephen b. March 15 : 1724—Silas b. Janr 11 : 1732–3 —Martin b. Febr. 15 : 1734–5—

Samuell brown & mercy brown m. August 13th : 1724—
Joseph prat & Editha Kellogg m. March ye 2d : 1727—
lois b. Decembr ye 13 : 1727—

William Chamberlin & Sarah Day m. Janewary ye 4th : 1710—William b. ye 22d day of Janewary 1711–12—Peleg b. Nouembr ye 25th—1713—John b. Janary 10 : 171⅖— Sarah was born—Marcy b.—Mary b.—

Lydya Daughter to Nathaniel Otis b. Janewary ye 20th : 1716—17—hannah b. februwary 29th : 1717—18—Dorothy b. Aprell ye 16th : 1721—Desier b. May ye 20th—1723— Nathaniel b. August ye 20th—1725—John b. Aprell ye 1t : 1728—(The next two births in the hand of Mr Bulkly viz.) Delight b. March 16 : 1730—Mercy b. July 3d : 1734—

Moses Rowlee & Martha Porter m. Septembr : 1707—Mary b. Decembr 15th—1708—Martha b. feby 11th—1710—11— Moses b. Septembr 5th—1714—Ann b. Aprell ye 5th : 1716—

Mary Daughter to James Kinion b. December 10th : 1722 —Abigaiel b. October 8th : 1724—

Easter Daughter to Daniell Chamberlin b. october ye 18th : 1722

Joseph Kellogg & Abigaill Miller m. Octobr 23d—1717— Joseph b. August the 8th : 1718—Daniell b. May ye 6th : 1720—Marcy b. May 20th : 1723—Moses b.—ye 10th Day : 1725—Elijah b. Janewary ye 15th—1728

John brown & Sarah haris m. August 13th : 1724—Sarah b. June 20th 1725—John b. Septembr 11th : 1727—

Jonathan Gillet & Sarah Eley m. Janewary 3d : 1717— Sarah b. Janewary ye 1t : 1718—Jonathan b. March 22d : 1720—Mary b. Decembr 13th—1723—Joseph b. Decembr

30th: 1725—Nehemiah b. March 1t: 1727-8—Jonah b. Aprell ye 10th: 1730—

ebenezer Day & Sarah tiffine ware m. februwary ye 3d: 1717-18—Deborah b. Nouembr ye 26t: 1718—Sarah b. July ye 12th: 1720—Jonathan b. Septem: 28: 1723—Jonathan Dyed August ye 18th; 1727—Ebenezer b. ye 28 Day of July, 1726—Silence b. June ye 1t: 1728—

lemewell son to Jonathan Daniels b. Aprell 6th: 1717—Jemima b. June 14th: 1720—

Easter Daughter to Daniell Chamberlin b. october 18th: 1722—Mahetable b. aprell 9th: 1725—Daniell b. Nouembr ye 2d: 1727—

James haris son of James haris b. Janeway 26th: 1719—thomas Lewis & Mary Rowlee m. feby 25th—1720—Shubaiel b. Decembr 6th: 1721—Sarah b. octobr ye 10: 1723—Abigaill b. nouembr 30th: 1724—Thomas b. octobr 14th: 1726—Mary b. octobr—1728—esther b. december 31: 1730—

Ebenezer Northam & Mary Glover m. Janeway ye 15th: 1718-19—Samuell b. october 29th: 1720

Daniell Jones & Mary Worthington m. october 13th: 1720—Mary b. May 16th: 1724—(the three next births in Mr Bulkley's hand, viz.) Amasai b. Octor 2d: 1726—Mary b. June 13: 1729—Abigail b. May 1: 1732—

Samuell Son to Daniell Landon b. februwary the 19th: 1723—John Strong & Abijah Chapell ware m. febuwary ye 5th: 172¾—John b. february ye 8th: 172⅘—Zebalon b. decembr 11th: 1726—loes b. nouember 22d. 1728—& Dyed Janewary ye 14th—1729—Darkis b. february ye 10th: 1729-30—

Noah Clark & Sarah Taintor m. June ye 10th—1719—Sarah b. februwary ye 19th: about break of day 1719, and Dyed—Sarah b. the 9th day of march 1721—Noah b. August ye 24th: 1722-3—Jerusha b. feby: 28th: 1724—Ezra b. ye 8th day of nouember 1725—elihu b. ye eighth day of Nouember 1727—Esther b. october ye fowrtenth 1729—

Nathaniel Gilbert & Mary bessel m. februwary the 8th: 1720—21. Mary b. Nouembr ye 19th: 1721: about one oj the clock in ye after noon—Samuell b. Janewary 31: 1724—about half an howr past thre of ye Clock in the morning.

Georg Saxton & Elizàbeth Dible m. Nouembr 21t: 1723 —Elizabeth b. Janawary 11th: 1724–5.

Jacob Lomis & hannah taylor ware m. march 22d: 1716— John Day Junr & Sarah Lomis m. August ye 20: 1725—Stephen tayler Dyed Janey: 3: 1718–19—

Ebenèzer son to Eben. Northam b. June 22d: 1721—timothy b. June 16th: 1723—Mary b. march ye 13th: 1725— Lidia Northam b. october ye 25: 1727—(the next entry by Mr Bulkley, viz. Elijah b. June 18: 1733.

hannah daughter to william brown b. Janewary 25th: 1718 —William b. october 7th: 1720—

Daniell Skiner & mary brown m. march 21t: 1728—Elijah b. Decembr 1t: 1728—

(The next two entries by Mr Bulkley, viz.) Jacob son to Daniel Worthington & Elizabeth his wife b. Feby 2d. 1735–6 —Sarah b. Novr: 27: 1734—

John Chapman & Sarah Carier m. Septembr ye 7th: 1707 —Jeane b. octobr ye 15: 1708—Sarah b. aprell ye 25th: 1710—Luse b. Nouemb: ye 8th: 1712—John b. Janewary ye 10th: 1714—15—Jason b. decembr ye 7th: 1716—James b. Janewary ye 31t: 1719—20—Abner b. March ye 5th: 1722—(The three next entries by Mr Bulkley, viz.) Ziporah b. april 22: 1724—Gideon b. July 26th: 1726—Delight b. Octor 16: 1725?—

William mariner & abigaiell Welles m. Janewary 27th: 1721—22—abigaiell b. March 4th: 1724—Ebenezer b. June 30th: 1726—Rachell & Sarah twins & Daughters b. June ye 14th: 1729 (The three next entries by Mr Buckly, viz) asa b. Octr 9: 1732—Ephraim b. Septr 26: 1735—Grace b. June 5th 1737.

fredom son to Joseph Chamberlin b. aprell ye 15th : 1705—
John b. Janewary 31t: 1707-8.

Dinah Daughter to Isreal Wyat & Sarah (Pratt, o. m. t.)
his wife b. Janewary 27—170$—Jerusiah b. Nouemb 25—
1711 & Dyed the 2d Day of decembr 1711—Isreall Wyatt
dyed in the 12th year of his age ˙on the 25th Day of June
1712—Mary daughter to Isreall Wyat b. Nouemb: ye 19:
1716.

Jabez Rowle & tabitha harris m. feby 20: 1724—tabitha b.
octobr : 20: 1724—Jabez b. Janewary ye 10th : 1726—

Daniell Worthington & elizabeth Lomis m. Janewary ye
3d : 1720—21—elizabeth b. July 24th : 1721—elias b. October 31st : 1722—Asa b. June 16th : 1724—Sibil b. aprell
19th : 1727—Samuel b. february 16th : 1728-9—Rhoda b.
Septmber ye 25th: 1730—(The next two entries by Mr Bulkley, viz.,) Mehitabell b. Febr 10th : 1731-2—Daniel b. august
18th : 1734—

Elizabeth daughter to Daniell Galusiah b. octobr ye 3d:
1719—Nathaniell Lomis & Sarah Skiner m. August ye 7th :
1721—Sarah b. Septembr ye 15th : 1722—

John Northam & hannah pumery m. may ye 9th: 1721—
hannah b. June ye 6th : 1722—Luranah b. may 25th : 1723—
(The next 7 entries by Mr Bulkley viz.,) Hannah b. May
29th, 1724—Jno. b. May 29 : 1725—Sarah b. August 6 :
1726—Ruhama & Ann twinns b. Octr 15 : 1727—Elizabeth
b. Aprill 20 : 1729—abigail b. Augt. 23 : 1731—Katherine
& Experience Twins b. Aprill 13 : 1733—

Sarah daughter to John Gold b. Aprell 24 : 1718—Sarah
daughter to Isaac Dauis b. June ye 3d: 1713—Isaac b. June
ye 13th: 1716—Jaell b. may ye 4th : 1718—easter b. Aprell
20th : 1720—

Benjamin Warner & Johana Strong m. March ye 17th:
1719—Samuell Gillet & Mary Chappell m. Janewary ye 30th :
1718—19—Samuell b. Aprell ye 20th : 1719—Isreall b. feb-

ruary ye 10th: 1721-2—Adonijah b. May ye 30th: 1724—
liphalet b. Noucmber ye 1t: 1726—liphelet Dyed August ye
22: 1728—Mary b. Aprell ye 11: 1729. (The next two by Mr
Bulkley, viz.,) Ruth b. Decembr 17th, 1731—Elilaphlet son to
Saml Gillit & Abigl his wife b. Aprill 29: 1734—William
Waters & margeret hills m. Janewary 13th: 1725—Joseph b.
June 2: 1726—

Caleb son to thomas Carrier b. october the 17th: 1715—
Isaac b. July the 5th: 1718—Rachell b. Septembr 15th:
1720—

John Carrier & mary brown m. July ye 22d: 1722—Abiall,
daughter b. may ye 7th: 1723—Sieble b. Nouembr 28th:
1725—Mary b. december 26t: 1727—(The last entry in the
hand of Mr. Bulkley, viz.,) Titus b. augt. 23: 1733.

John Weles & elizabeth Chamberlin m. Septembr 8th:
1715—Mary b. July 15th: 1716—John b. Nouembr 24th:
1718—

ebenezer Skiner & Sarah Taylor m. March 17th: 1725—
Sarah b. Janewary 10th: 1725-6—Elizabeth b. July 17th:
1727—Ebenezer b. May ye 14th: 1729 (The last entry in
Mr Bulkley's hand, viz.) Mary b. March 17: 1736-7—

hepsibah Daughter to Samuell Spencer b. Decembr ye 8th:
1701—Samuell b. March ye 8th: 1704—William b. August
ye 9th: 1708—Edward b. Aprell 29th: 1711—Sarah b. Septemb ye 14: 1714—Caleb b. June ye 28th: 1718—

ann Daughter to John holmes b. June ye 1t: 17—Dorothy
b. august ye 14th: 1726—Elizabeth the wife of John holms
Dyed Decembr ye 14th: 1726—

Josiah Gillett & Sarah pellet m. March 7th: 1711—Josiah
b. Nouembr 11th: 1712, & Dyed october ye 13: 1714—Daniell b. februwary 2d: 1714—Josiah b. decemb. ye 7th: 1715
—Sarah b. June 24th: 1717—Dauid b. June ye 30th: 1719
—elizabeth b. aprell ye 15th: 1721—timothy b. June 27th:
1723—Mary b. March 3d: 1725 & Dyed ye 17th: day of
aprell next following—

Noah pumery was b. unto Joseph Pumery & hannah his wife may ye 19th: 1700—

John Lord & hannah ackley m. Decembr 25th: 1718— Sarah b. aprell ye 17th: 1721—John b. march ye 3d: 1722-3 —hannah ye wife of John Lord Dyed March ye 3d: 1722-8—

Josiah Gates & Grace Rathbon m. the 9th: Day of may 1714—Mary b. July 3d: 1715—Abigaiell b. August ye 13th: 1719—hannah b. Septr ye 5th: 1721—Josiah b. Janewary 15th: 1722-3—Thomas b. July ye 3d: 1724—Grace b. october ye 8th: 1725—(The next two entries by Mr. Bulkley, viz.,) Elizabeth b. May 8th: 1729—Samll b. Decr 26: 1730.

James Roberds & Rebecah Daylee m. Nouembr 1718. Rebecah b. Janewary 3d: 1719-20—Edenah Daughter, b. May 11th: 1722. James b. September ye 9th: 1724—Elenah b. Janewary 9th: 1727—

Micaiell Taintor & Vniss foot ware Married Decembr ye 3d: 1712—Vniss b. Aprell ye 13th: 1717—Micaiell Taintor son to Micaiell Taintor was born decembr 31st: 1719—Charles b. feby 8th: 1722-3—John b. July 23d: 1725—Mary b. Nouembr ye 6th: 1727—prudence b. Decembr 9th: 1729— (The two next entries by Mr. Bulkley, viz.,) Sarah b. Aprill 3d: 1731—Ann b. Octobr 21: 1734—(The next entry is in the hand of Deac. Aaron Skinner, viz.,) Ann their Daughter departed this Life Jan ye 31st: 1755—

William Williams & Dorothy Jonson m. october 21t: 1713 —William b. october 13th: 1714—Elizabeth b. March 13th: 1716—John b. July 22d: 1718—Margery b. July 5th: 1720 —Isaac b. July ye 16th: 1728—

Alice daughter to James newton b. ye 28th: Day of februwary 1686—James b. ye third day of aprell 1690—Anne b. aprell the 13th: 1692—Isreall b. ye 5th: Day of March: 1694.

Samuell Lomis & elizabeth holmes m. decemb 12th: 1717. John addams & Ruth Lomis m. June ye 20th: 1708—Samuell b. Janewary ye 26: 1713-14—Ruth b. Janewy ye 28th: 1715-16—Joseph b. august 26th: 1717—David b. Decembr

13th: 1719—Mary b. July ye 9th: 1726—Andrew b. october ye 2d: 1728—Elizabeth b. Decembr 21: 1730—Rachell b. Septr 1: 1732—Hannah b. Octobr 5th—1733——(The last 3 entries by Mr. Bulkley).

Ecabod Chapman & Abigaiell Clother m. July 4th: 1723—abigaiell b. march ye 10th: 1724—Irene b. februwary ye 2d; 1724-5—Ann b. february 27th: 1726-7—(The three next entries by Mr. Bulkley, viz.,) Irene b. May ye 4th: 1729—Ichabod b. Septr 28th: 1732—Elisha b. Decr 13th: 1735—Lydia b. Septemr 15th: 1738—

Jonathan Wells & mary Newton m. July ye 11th: 1717—Jonathan b. Aprell ye 13th: 1718—Simion b. June 17th: 1720—Rubin b. May ye 23d: 1722—Mary b. Septembr 14th: 1724—Irene b. May ye 4th: 1729.

Sarah daughter to James harris b. Septr ye 27th: 1697—James b. Jane'y 26th: 1699—mary b. Nouemb: 1t: 1702—Jonathan b. June ye 15th: 1705—Alph b. feby 29th: 1708—& Died August ye 30th: 1708—Abigaill b. may 17th: 1711—Lebeus b. August 11th: 1713—Alph b. august 31t: 1716. Delight b. octobr ye 17th: 1720—

hannah Daughter to enos Randall b. nouembr ye 1t: 1717—Joseph b. august ye 5th: 1721—Dauid b. August 21t: 1724—

hannah Daughter to ebenezer palmeter b. August 22d: 1720—ebenezer b. may 10th: 1723—

Jonathan Northam & mary day m. Decembr 20: 1722—mary b. nouem: 28th: 1723—Jonathan b. August 29th: 1725—Dorothy b. march ye 17th: 1727—Asa b. decembr ye 4th: 1728—(The next entry is by Deac. Aaron Skinner, viz., Grace b. January 24th: 1731—

ephreaim foot & Sarah Chamberlin 'm. June 1708—Margerit b. may ye 13th: 1711—Sarah b. octobr 20th: 1713—Ephreaim b. Aprell 27th: 1716—

Isaac Jones & hannah weles m. July 11th: 1717—Joel b.

93

August 29: 1718—Elijah b. Janewary 21st: 1719 20—hannah b. March 12th: 1721—Isaac b. June 19: 1722—More of
Isaac Jones children are Recorded in ye 3d book of Records—
—mary daughter to James tredway & Sarah his wife b. July
ye 15th: 1709—Sarah b. Aprell 15th: 1711—Lydia Janey
16th: 1714—eunice Nouembr ye 4th: 1717—Lois b. febey
2d: 1720—Elijah b. aprell ye 8th: 1722—Anne b. March
9th: 1724—Abigaiel b. may 29th: 1726—

Joseph pepoon & mary Dibell m. December ye 12th: 1717
Joseph b. may 20th: 1719—mary b. aprell 18th: 1721—Silas
b. Janewary ye 5th: 1722 3—mary the wife of Joseph pepoon Dyed feby 23d: 1724—Joseph pepoon & mary thomas
m. Janewary 13th: 1725—elizabeth b. october ye 10th: 1725
—Joseph Dyed october ye 20th: 1725—mary Dyed october
ye 23d: 1725—marcy b. Septembr 25th: 1727—Sarah &
Ruth b. December 30: 1728 & Sarah Dyed March 31t:
1729—

abigaiell Daughter to John Clother b. Nouembr 30th: 1704
—John b. Janewary 3d: 1707—Sarah b. March 13th: 1709.
Anne b. March 8th: 1711—Barbra b. Decembr 3d: 1714—
Elizabeth b. Nouembr 29th: 1716—Mary b. Septemb 10th:
1717-18—Lucrese b. June 20th: 1720—

James tredway Dyed May 26th: 1728 in ye 52d year of
his age—

John bigelow son to John bigelow b. March 25th: 1709—
hannah the wife of John bigelow Dyed March 31t: 1709—
John bigelow abouesd & Sarah Bigelow m. Nouember 4th:
1709. Sarah b. July 17th: 1712—Jonathan b. may 21t:
1714—Asa b. September 3d: 1720

ansess Daughter to Isreall Newton b. the first Day of Janewary 1716—mary b. march 1t: 1719—hannah b. June 28:
1721—abigaiell b. octobr 17th: 1723—

Isaac phelps son to Josiah phelps Dyed february ye 25th:
1715—16—zefaniah Dyed Aprell ye 10th:—1716—Josiah b.
Septm: 1717—

Isaac Rowlee & hannah harris m. may ye 30th: 1717—Retern b. august 26th: 1719—harris b. august ye 1t: 1721—thomas b. March ye 4th: 1723—Isaac b. September ye 8th: 1725.

Ruth Daughter to nathaniell Lomis b. August ye 21: 1713 —timothy son to Joseph pepoon b. August ye 19th: 1730—Hannah Daughter to benjamin Lewes b. Aprell 7th: 1717—Mary b. June ye 17th: 1720—

Azariah pratt & hannah Coleman m. may ye 5th: 1725—hannah b. June ye 8th: 1726—Lucresee b. feby 8th: 1727–8 —Azariah b. feby 25th: 1729–30—(The next two entries by Mr. Bulkley, viz.,) Sarah b. Octr 16th: 1732—Abigail b. Jan. 8: 1733–4—

Samuel Northam Dyed the 12th Day of Nouember 1726—

Gesham son to Isaac fox b. December 23d: 1716—Gidian b. october 24th: 1719—

phillep Cauerlee & hannah addams m. Decembr 20th: 1713 —Next, in another hand is " Sarah ye wife of John Swetland Who was ye widow Treadway, Deseased: February 28th: 1753—Old Stile—

may ye 7th or thare abouts in ye year 1717 we whose Names are underunto subscribed saw a bay mare L upon ye shoulder D C vpon buttock white hairs in her forehead: we saw this mare In a suffering Condistion : & taken up by Jonathan Cutler & prised by Mathew Rowlee & John pendall at thirty shillings—Mathew Rowlee John pendall—the aboue brought to me to record by Jonathan Cutler—entered may 18th 1717—

Colchester June ye 10th: 1718—John Calkin Joshua Tileson & noah phelps all of hebron Brought to me the subscriber thre stone horses which are not lawful to run in the Comons as thay say—one of them a bay hors about thre years old: branded on the shoulder with this figur 4: & L on the near buttock—a black list on his back—about 12 hands and two

yenches in hight—another bay hors branded 4 on 'ye near
shoulder—12 hands & one eyench in height about thre years
old :—the other is also a bay ston hors of two years old as thay
say : with a small star side of ye of ear In the forehead :
Branded on ye near shoulder with this figur—U marked with
a half peny on ye side—in height 12 hands—I saw the height
of said horses measured : & the height Colour & brand Are
as abousaid—

Test Micaiell Taintor Justice of Peace—

Colchester June ye 9th : 1719 : ebenezer Day of Colchester
brought to me the subscriber : a brownish black stone horse of
about two years old : so Judged : he Saith taken up in the
Comons : & not Lawfull to go in the Comons ; said horse is
branded with Colchester town brand on the shoulder : a littell
white on the off hind foot—I saw him Measured : & his height
is twelue hands and about thre quarters of an eynch—

Test—Micaiell Taintor Justice of peace—

Colchester August ye 27th : 1719—John Gold brought to
me ye subscriber a brown stone horse of two years old, he
saith taken up in the Comons : not Lawfull to go on the Comons being but twelue hands & thre eynches in height (as he
saith) sd horse is branded with Colchester brand on the near
shoulder : & the same brand on the Ribs—

Micaiell Taintor Justice of peace—

februwary the 13th : 1719—20—John Day of Colchester—
hath taken vp a dark brown mare with a few white hares on
her forehead : with a bay mare Colt : about six months old—the
mare is branded on the left shoulder with Colchester town brand
—taken up as strays—in a suffering Condistion—and apprised
at forty shillings by Andrew Carrier & Micaiell Taintor Junr.

Know all men by these presents that I Joshua fairbanks of the town of Rentom within her Majesties prouince
of the Masachusets Bay in Newengland for & in Considera-

tion of the sum of thirty & seauen pownds to me Well and
truly paid by Robert Ransom of the towne of Colchester in
the County of hartford within her Majesties Colony of Conetecot in Newengland aforesaid tharewith I do acknolig myself
fully Satisfied & Contented & by these presents do exonerate
acquit & Dischaŕge the said Robert Ransom his heigrs executors & administrators for euer by these presents haue Giuen
Granted bargained Sold Assined Set ouer & by these presents
do for my self My heigrs executors & administrators fully frely
and absolutely Grant Assine set ouer & Confirm unto the said
Robert Ransom his heigrs executors administrators & assigns
one hundred acres of Land mentioned in the Deed from John
addams on the other side acording as it is Bounded & butted
on the other side & euery part thareof as it is thare prescribed
without any Molestation from me or any person from By or
under me or from any other person Lawfully Claiming the
same or any part thareof: for the Confirmation of the 'prem-
ces I the said Joshua fairbanks haue set to my hand & seal
this fowrth Day of Nouembr: in the tweluth Year of her
Majesties Reign—Joshua fairbanks (＊＊＊)
   Ano: Domini 1713

Signed Sealed and Deliuered in the presents of vs witneses
            MIOAIELL TAINTOR JAMES NEWTON—

Entered on Record, The Date abouesaid

Nouembr ye 4th: ano: Dom. 1713—Joshua fairbanks the
Granter appeared In Colchester Before me the subscriber one
of her Majesties Justices of the peace for the County of hartford & acknowliged The aboue written Instrument to be his
fre & volentary act & Deed—
               MICAIELL TAINTOR Justice

   Susanah Daughter to William Chapman was b. february
28th: 1715—16—Mary b. Jenewary 20th : 1717—8, abagaiell
b. June ye 28: 1720—ebenezer b. March 22: 1724—Wil-

liam Chapman & marcy Chapman wer m. Decembr 19th: 1728—William Chapman had a daughter born & Dyed Janawary 3d—1730—

Sarah Daughter to John Clark was b. August 13: 1723—Johanah b. february: 1725-6 & Dyed Nouembr ye 5th—1729—John b. September 22d: 1728—(The next two entries in the hand of Mr. Bulkley, viz.,) Joanna Daughter to Jno. Clark and mindwell his wife b. July 4th 1731—Nathaniell b. Febr. 17th: 1733-4—

Samell son to Isaac Jones was b. aprell ye 22—1724—Lydia b. Nouember ye 14th: 1725—William b. September 18th: 1727—Esekiell b. March ye 22d, 1729—(The next seven by Mr. Bulkley, viz.,) Nathan b. Decr. 30th: 1731—Asa b. Oct. 16th: 1733—Eunice March 10th: 1735—Sarah, Feb. 16th: 1736—Mary b. July 27: 1737—Lemuel b. Octr. 18: 1739—Josiah b. Jany 20th: 1740-1

Noah Coleman & mercy wright ware maried march ye 5th —1730.

Joseph prat & editha kellogg ware married march ye 2d, 1727—Lois b. the 13th Day of Decemb 1727—Lydiah b. March ye 3d, 1730—(The next two entries by Mr. Bulkley, viz.,) Joseph b. August 2d, 1732—Peter b. Febr. 8th, 1734-5—

Sarah Daughter to John rowle b. Janewary 1722—Deborah b. Decembr ye 14th: 1725—John b. July ye 7th: 1727 —Seth b. May ye 6th 1730—

Timothy Carier and frances Cripin m. ye 26th Day of february 1729-30—

Grace daughter to William Dickson & Rebecca his wife b. March 12th, 1721—John son to William Dickson b. Nouember 12th, 1722—William b. may ye 12th: 1724—Rebecah b. Janewary 12th, 1725—Margaret b. August 18th, 1727—& Dyed Nouember 18: 1728—

timothy b. May ye 5th 1730----(The next by Mr. Bulkley, viz.) Thomas b. May 3d, 1733—

Lidia daughter to Joseph Chamberlin b. October 20th: 1721—Joseph b. aprell ye 11th, 1724—Job b. feby the 8th, 1725–6—Jonathan b. July ye 1st Day & Dyed ye last day of September being thre month old : 1729—another son named Jonathan b. february 22d, 1729–30 and Dyed march ye 3d, next after—Lidiah the wife of Joseph Chamberlin Dyed March 3d,—1730—

John son of John niles b. March 25—1718—nathan son to John niles b. february ye 20 : 1720—Samll b. march 13 : 1722 and Dyed in Augst 1726—nathan b. may ye 7th 1724— Mary b. June 26th 1726—thomas b. September 28th 1728— Abigaiell b. Septem ye 4th 1730—

noah pumery & elizabeth Randall ware m. ye 25th day of December 1728 & a Daughter born to Joseph pumery february ye 29th & Dyed toward the latter end of Decembr next after—

Simion son to James Crocker b. September ye 19th 1722— Abigaiell b. March 22d, 1724—hannah b. Janewary 17th: 1726 —levy b. may ye 11th 1728—Jonathan b. March 16th 1730— (The next four by Mr. Bulkley, viz.) James b. Aprill 20th 1732—Thankfull b. Jan. 27th, 1733–4—Lydia b. Jan. 14th, 1735–6—Ephraim b. Septr 21 : 1739—

John hopson & lydiah kellogg ware m. may 28th, 1730—

Samuell Landon son of Daniell Landon was b. February 19th—1723—Deborah b. february 16th 1725—William b. Aprill 25 : 1727—Joshua b. aprell 13th—1729—

Ebenezer thomas & unice strong ware maried decembr ye 7th : 1730—

Caleb Lomis & Joanah Skiner ware m. fery (Feb. c. m. t.) 28 : 1728–9—Caleb b. Nouember ye 28th, 1729—

Daniell skiner & elizabeth hitchcock ware maried Decembr ye 22 : 1727—Daniell b. februwary ye last Day 1728.-9—

(The next seven entered by Mr. Bulkley, viz.,) Elisabeth b. March 22—1733—Sarah b. Novr. 25 : 1735—John b. Augt. 17 : 1738—Elijah b. June 8th, 1742—Hannah b. May 26— 1745—Lydia b. Octr 15—1747—Rubin b. Augt 8th, 1750: Lydia died June ye 26th 1753—

James tredway & Sarah mun ware maried June ye 4th— 1729—

hezakiah kilburn & ann Clother ware m. ye 25th Day of December—1728—hezekiah b. ye 1t Day of December 1729 (The two next entries by Mr. Bulkley, viz.,)Asa b. Janr 26 : 1731--2—Ann b. March 25 : 1734—

Lefnt. John holmes & Ann Rockwell m. Decembr ye 3d, 1729.

thomas son to samuell brown was b. ye 9th of Novr. 1724 —Ruth b. Nouember ye 2d : 1726—kesiah b. December ye 5th 1728—(The next by Mr. Bulkley, viz.,) Amos b. Decemr 1st, 1730—

Nathan Williams & elizabeth Lewis ware m. Septbr 16 : 1725—Abraham b. July 21 : 1726—elizabeth b. March 30 : 1729—

Nathaniel Kellogg & elizabeth Wiliams ware m. July ye— 1725—Charles b. ye 17th Day of September 1726—elizabeth b. July ye 8—1729—(The next three by Mr. Bulkley, viz.,) Sarah b. Febr 22d, 1732—Delight b. Octr 5th 1734—Margarett b. Janr. 17 : 1736--7—

John Dugles & elizabeth quiterfield ware m. Janewary 27th : 1728—Mary b. Nouembr 29th : 1729—

benjamin quiterfield & unice kellogg ware m. July ye 11th : 1728—benjamin b. Aprell 22—1729—(The next four by Mr. Bulkley, viz.,) Eunice b. Febr. 26 : 1730--1—Asa b. June 28 : 1733—Israell b. August 28th : 1735—Hannah b. Novr. 3d, 1737 & Dyed Dec. 10th, 1738—

Cornelious fuller & patience Chappell ware maried february ye 25th 1730—

John bebe son to John bebee was b. December ye 5th 1727 —hesekiah b. September ye 26th—1729----

Asariah Lomis and Abigaiell Newton ware m. Decembr
25th: 1723—Dimis b. Septembr 5th—1724—(The next two
entries by Deac. Aaron Skiner, viz.,) Silence b. January ye
6th, 1737—Lieut Azariah Lomis Departed this Life February
ye 9th A. D. 1758—

Judah Lewes & Sarah Kellog m. february ye 19th: 1728–
9—Sarah b. Janey 18th: 1729–30. (The next five entries
by Mr. Bulkley, viz.,) The Rev'd Mr Judah Lewis & Mercy
Kellog m. Decr. 24: 1734—Ephraim b. October 4th 1735—
Lydia b. Febr 21: 1736–7—Judah b. March 14: 1738–9—
The Rev'd Mr Judah Lewis Dyed April 15th 1739—(The
next entry by Deac. Skiner, viz.,) Lydia d. sept. the 12th
1748—

Nathaniell kellogg & Elizabeth Williams ware m. ye 1st:
Day of July 1725—Charles b. the 17th Day of Septembr
1726—Elizabeth b. ye 8th Day of July 1729—(The next by
Mr. Bulkley, viz.,) Sarah b. Febr. 22: 1731–2.

Elizabeth Daughter to Jonathan kilburn was b. octobr ye
15th—1713—

Elizabeth Daughter to John hitchcock was b. may the 3d:
1708—Eliakim b. febrewary ye 14th: 1712–13—hannah
b. october ye 29: 1717—Easter b. Septembr 1720—

Elizabeth Daughter to Charles Williams was b. febrewary
13th: 1702—

Jonathan son to Jonathan kilburn was b. June ye 8th: 1707
—hesekiah b. Nouemb: ye 2d: 1708—

Shubaiell Rowlee & hannah Brown ware Maried may ye
8th: 1709—a Daughter b. Decembr 12: 1716 & Dyed ye
10th of Janewry following—experianc b. august ye 8th:
1718—Mathew b. october ye 5th: 1720—patienc b. August
ye 16th: 1723—marcy b. Aprell ye 30th: 1710—hannah b.
March ye 10th: 1712—Elizabeth b. october 3d: 1714—

Joseph son to Noah Colman b. June 28th: 1706—Noah
Colman Dyed Nouembr ye 7th: 1711—

Joseph son to John day b. September ye 27th: 1702—Benjamin b. febrewary ye 7th: 1703-4----Eaditha b. septemb: 10th: 1705----Daniell b. March ye 9th: 1709 ---Dauid b. July ye 18th: 1710---Abraham b. March ye 17th: 1712----Isaac b. May 17th: 1713----

Andrew Carrier & mary addams ware m. Janewary ye 11th: 1704-5—Andrew b. febrewary 2d: 1705-6—John b. June ye 14th: 1707—Mary b. Aprell 19th: 1708—thomas b. June ye 20th: 1711—Benjamin b. Septemb: 17: 1713—Kuff Isreall Newton's Negroman: & the Indian woman named Sarah ware m. as he saith: March ye—1716—martha Daughter to the—said Kuff & Sarah his wife b. Janewary ye 25th: 1719—

Ebenezer Dibels daughter Elizabeth was b. august ye 8th: 1701—Mary ye wife of ebenezar Dibell dyed septemb 24th: 1703—ebenezar Dibell & An hooton ware Married agust 29th: 1706—Ann b. June 27: 1708·—Ann the wife of ebenezer Dibell dyed the 22d: of July 1708.

Ebenezer Dibell & mary lewess ware m. Decem. 30th: 1708.

Jeames brown dyed may the 8th: 1704—

Nathaniell Skiner & mary gillet ware m. June 13th: 1706 —Nathaniell was b. July 10th: 1707---Mary b. July 10th: 1709----thomas b. Aprell ye 6th: 1712----(The next three entries by Mr. Bulkley, viz.:) Eunice daughter to Decon Nathll Skiner & mary his wife b. Decembr 15--1715----David son of ye aforesd persons b. Jan. 7th: 1717—and died on Janr 31st, Item: David b. Novr 6th 1719----

Samuell son to thankfull brown was b. decembr the 5th—1703—

Elizabeth Daughter to Josiah Strong was b. the 21 of october 1705----Mary b. Septemb ye 19th: 1707----Josiah b. Septembr ye 9th: 1709—uniss b. Nouembr ye 19: 1711—Caleb b. the 20th: Day of february 1713-14—Rachell b. Aprell ye 21t: 1716—Dorothy b. may 25th: 1718—

ebenezer kellogg & Mabell Butler were m. July ye 6th: 1706—Abigaiell was b. June 25th: 1707—Ebenezer b. Jane-

9*

wary 30th : 1709—10—elizabeth b. Septr 25th : 1712—Mary
b. June ye 3d, 1715—prudence b. Decembr 24th : 1717—

John son to John Jonson b. Jeneway ye 16th : 1712—13—
Dauid b. february 10th : 1715—16—elijah b Septembr 20th :
1718—Elizabeth februwary 17th : 1720—21—Elisha b. July
16th : 1724—

Joshua son to Josiah Strong b. July 20th 1720—Irena b.
octobr ye 20th : 1722—Asahell b. June 22d : 1725—

Daniell Clark & elesebeth butler m. the 4th : Day of Decemb : 1704—hannah b. June 30th : 1706—elisabeth b. June
29 : 1708—Daniell b. Septembr 28th : 1711—a son b. July
17th : 1710 & dyed the same Day—Jonah b. Deeembr ye
19th : 1713—Roger b. Decembr 24th : 1715—Alexander b.
Nouembr ye 6th : 1717—Zuruiah b. March ye 14th : 1719—
mabell b. octobr ye 7th : 1721—

hannah Daughter to ephream weles was b. Jeneway ye 2d :
1709—10—Lidiah b. Jeneway ye 18th : 1711—12—R
beckah b. Septemb ye 1t : 1715—

Rebeckah Daughter to Danll Clark b. Jun : ye 16th : 1726—
Darius b. febwary the 2d : 1719—20—Uriah b. Nouembr 2d :
1722—

ebenezar son of ebenezar skiner b. August ye 8th : 1703—
Sarah b. Agust 6t : 1705—Joseph b. Jenewary 17th : 1707–8
—Deborah b. August 24th : 1710—Gidion b. October 19th :
1712—Abigaiell b. July 9th : 1715—Ann b. Septembr ye
8th : 1717—Mary b. septembr 18th : 1719—

Joseph prat & Sarah Colyer ware m. July 22d : 1697—
Joseph b. June 30th : 1698—asariah b. decemb. 7th : 1699—
Abigaiel b. Nouembr 30th : 1702—Ruth b. March 16th :
1705—6—elisha b. Agust ye 10th : 1707—Daniell b. May ye
26th : 1710—Sarah b. August ye—1713—

Timothy son to ebenezer skiner b. July 10th : 1721—Lydia
b. Aprell ye 20th : 1723—margaritt b. December 28th : 1725—

Samuell son of Samuell brown b. Decemb ye 12th : 1718.

Samuell dyed october 5 : 1719—elizabeth b. Nouembr ye 16th : 1720—Samuell b. March 10 : 1723—

Deborah daughter to Thomas Day dyed october 20th : 1703 Samuell son to Thomas Day b. Septemb 15th : 1704—the Wife of John day Dyed May 12th : 1714—

John son to Robert Ransom b. Nouember ye 13th : 1709— Mary b. August ye 30th : 1711—James b. March 13th :— 1713—Joshua b. may ye 3d : 1715—Robert b. March 25th : 1717—alce (daughter) b. Septembr 6th : 1719—Newton b. februwary ye 21t : 1722—Peleg b. September ye 20th : 1724 —Amos b. februwary ye 17th : 1727—

Benjamin son of clemenc kithophell was b. Aprell 11th : 1704—Richard b. Septemb : 27th : 1706—elizabeth b. June 3d : 1709—John b. Septembr 3d : 1711—Colings son to Clement kiterfield b. Nouembr ye 9th : 1720—

Asariah son to Decon Samull Lomis b. may ye 2d : 1700— elisabeth b. Nouemb : 13th : 1702—Sarah b. March ye 7th : 1705—Caleb b. Septemb. ye 20th : 1707—Daniell b. febrewary 20th : 1708—9—

Abigaiell Daughter to James Mun b. october 17 : 1700— James son to James Mun & mary his wife b. febrewary 2d : 1703—hannah b. March 26th : 1706—Sarah b. June 28th : 1708—

kasiah Daughter to Thomas Brown b. September 22d : 1707—Samuell brown & elisabeth Collins ware m. may ye 12th : 1713—

John addams son to John addams Junr b. August 21t : 1709—Daniell b. febrewary ye 12th, 1711—

Mary Butler Dyed march 19th : 1715—

Samuell kellogg Dyed August 24th : 1708—

Remembrance Daughter to Richard Carier b. Aprell ye 14th : 1715—Sarah Daughter to Richard Carier dyed Septembr 27 : 1717—

Mary the wife of Decon Thomas Skiner Dyed March 26th : 1704—

Benjamin son to henry tomseon b. Jun 19th: 1709—Isaac
b. Aprell 20th : 1711—thankfull b. Aprell 17th : 1713—

Sarah Daughter to the Reurent mr John bulkly b. aprell
8th : 1702—about the middell of the afternoone—another
daughter was born May 6th : 1704 & dyed about 3 howrs after
its birth—John bulkley was b. aprell 19 : 1705 about 3 howrs
before day—Dorothy b. feby. 28 : 1706—Geshom b. febrewary ye 4th : 1708–9—Charels b. decembr 26th : 1710—peter
b. Nouembr 21t : 1712—patience b. march 21—1715 about
noone—oleuer b. July 29th : 1717—lucee b. Janewary 29th :
1719—20, about break of Day—Irene & Joseph (twins) son
and daughter to mr bulkley b. feb. 10th : 1721–2 about two
hours before day—Irene dyed ye 20th of ye same month following about two howrs before daye—Joseph Dyed ye 25th
of ye same month following about ye daun of ye day—

Dinah daughter to henry tomeson b. februwary ye 18th—
1718–19—elesebeth Daughter to John hitchcock b. May 23d :
1708—thomas Brown senr Dyed Aprell ye 18th : 1717—Shubaiell Rowlee Dyed March the 28th : 1714—

Daniell son to Samuell Brown & elizabeth Colings his wife
b. June ye 12 : 1714—elizabeth ye wife of Samuell Brown
Dyed July ye 2d : 1714—Samuell Brown & presilla kent
ware m. Aprell ye 11th : 1715—Dauid b. March ye 29th :
1716—look on ye top of the other side for more—

John fuller son to Samuell fuller b. Nouember the 3d :
1704—Samuell b. the last day of agust 1706—Moses b. Jenewary the 30 : 1708—Aron b. June ye 3d : 1711—Mahitable
b. august 6 : 1716—marcy b. June ye 27 : 1718—Mary b.
febry : ye 28 : 1721—desire b. february 2d : 1723—abner b.
Decembr ye 10th : 1724.—(daughter, b. June 1727—

1699 in July 22d : Timothy Carier son of Richard Carrier
was b.—Sarah b. aprell ye 13th : 1701—Mahitabell b. aprell
16 : 1702—elisabeth, the wife of Richard Carier Dyed March
ye 6 : 1704—Richard Carier & thankfull Brown ware M.

July 29th: 1707—hannah b. May ye 1t: 1708—amos son to Richard Carier b. July ye 3d: 1722.

Lydia Daughter of Samuell Gilbert b. Septembr 4th: 1707 —Mercy b. Octobr 4th: 1709—

William Roberds & elisebeth Northam ware m. ye 20th: of July 1705—samll: b. febrewary ye 8th: 1705-6—An b. March ye 8th: 1707-8 Sarah b. Septm: 13th: 1710—Jerusha b. Janewary 31: 1713—William b. March ye 4th: 1715 lemewell b. march 24th: 1717—Mary b. aprell 1st: 1721— elizabeth ye wife of William Roberds Dyed August ye 22d: 1728—

Caleb Jefferis & hannah parsons the reputed daughter to Jonathan parsons late of Northampton deceased ware m. Decembr ye 17th: 1710—

Nathaniell foot & ann Clark m. July ye 4th: 1711.

Daniell son to Josiah phelps b. Decembr the 17th: 1704— Ann b. febreary 8th: 1708-9—Isaac b. febrewary 1t: 1710-11 —Zefeniah b. Nouembr 7th: 1712—elizabeth b. may 16th: 1715—

Nathaniell son of Nathaniell kellogg b. May ye 8th: 1703 —Sarah b. Decembr 27th: 1707—Lydya b. May 29th: 1710 —ezra b. Septembr ye 6th: 1724—

Marcy Daughter to Isaac bigloo b. July 23d: 1711 & dyed about 3 months after—Isack son to Isaac biglo b. may 4th: 1713—marcy b. february 4th: 1715—Mary b. July 31t: 1719 —Samuell b. the 21t Day of December 1724—Sarah b. the the 27th: day of June 1727—lidia b. aprell the 22d: 1729— (In another place) hannah b. ye 2d; Day of octobr: 1721— abigaiell b. Aprell 13th: 1723—

thankful Daughter to Richard Carier b. aprell 29th, 1711—

(Here ends the recording of births, marriages and deaths by Micaiell Taintor Esq.—What follows is chiefly in the hand of Esq. Bulkley—A small portion of it is in the hand of Capt. Aaron Skinner--)" Mary daughter of Daniel & Elizabeth Worth-

ington was b. Augt. 2d: 1737—Telitha b. Nov. 25: 1738—
Abigail b. March 10: 1740—Almy b. april 12: 1741—Mehi-
tabel b. June 27: 1742 & dyed July 1: 1742—William b.
oct. 20: 1743 & d. March 4th 1744—William b. Jan. 29;
1744-5—Amasai b. April 16: 1746—

Susannah daughter to Joseph Isham b. 14: Feb. 1737-8.

Samuel Kellogg & Abigail Sterling, m. Jan. 8th, 1735-6—
Abigail b. Oct. 29: 1736—Samuel b. Dec. 20: 1738—Hannah b. Sept. 30: 1740—Ann b. Novr 30: 1742—Mary b.
April 27: 1745, New Stile—Eunice b. Feb. 26: 1747—Daniel
b. June 1: 1749—Ann d. July 9: 1758, in the 16th year of
her age—

Martha daughter to Isaac Crocker & Elisabeth his wife b.
March 3: 1731—Abigail b. March 10: 1733—a daughter
(still born Sept. 26: 1736—

Elisha Pratt & Ann Porter m. Feb. 27: 1735-6—Elisha
b. Jan. 25: 1735-6—David b. April 30: 1738—

Gershom Bulkley & Abigail Robins m. Nov. 27: 1733—
Sarah b. Nov. 10: 1735—

Noah Wells & Sarah Wyatt were m. Aprill 15: 1714—
Israell Wyatt b. Dec. 17; 1714—Jerusha b. Jan. 6: 1716-17
& d. Dec. 17: 1717—Noah b. Sept. 25: 1718—Sarah b. Jan.
12: 1721-2—David b. Sept. 10: 1723—Moses b. Oct. 3: 1725
—Gideon b. Jan. 22: 1728-9—Silas b. July 8: 1730—Jerusha
b. Jan. 28: 1733-4—Amos b. Feb. 28: 1735—

Mary wife of Ebenezer Dibble d. March 5: 1736—Elisa-
beth daughter of Benjamin Carrier & Elisabeth his wife b.
Nov. 25: 1735—Hannah daughter to Joseph Pumery &
Elisabeth his wife b. April 28: 1734—John Daley son to
Joseph Daley & Patience his wife b. Dec. 11: 1708—The
Revd Mr Joseph Lovett & Ann Holms m. Aprill 3: 1734—
Samuel b. Jan. 12: 1734-5—Benjamin Carrier & Elisabeth
Kneeland m. Feb. 6th 1734-5—Thomas Carrier Dyed May
16: A. D. 1735 aged about 108 or 109 years.

{ Isaac Bigloe & Abigail Skinner were m. March 14 : 1734
—Abigail b. Jan. 1: 1734–5—Ann b. March 7 : 1736—Isaac
b. Nov. 17: 1737—Timothy b. Nov. 18: 1739—Amasai b.
Dec. 28: 1741—& d. Jan. 18: following—Mary b. Feb. 2:
1743—Lydia b. May 2: 1745—Margarett b. Aug. 2: 1747—
Jerusha b. March 8: 1748–9—Rubey b. Dec. 14: 1750—
Samuel b. Nov. 1: 1752—Amasai b. Feb. 11: 1755—Addi
(a son) b. Oct. 18: 1757—Ruby d. June 5: 1759—

Nathaniel son to Joshua Cole & Mary his wife b. Jan. 31:
1734–5—

David Bigloe & Editha Day m. Dec. 11: 1729—Hannah
b. Nov. 11: 1730—David b. May 7: 1732—Amasa b. Sept.
3: 1733—Ezra b. April 10: 1736—Daniel b. May 25: 1738.,
Eli b. August 25: 1739—Azariah b. Dec. 26: 1741—Editha
b. March 16: 1744—Editha wife of David Bigelow d. Jan.
19: 1746—David Bigelow & Marcy Lewis m. Jan. 21: 1747
—Stephen b. Oct. 27: 1747—Stephen d. Sept. 13: 1748—
Stephen b. June 5: 1749—Moses b. Oct. 4: 1750, & d. Dec.
23: 1750—Stephen d. Aug. 5: 1751—Eli d. Aug. 10: 1751
—Marcy b. Nov. 23: 1753—

Benjamin Chamberlin & Hannah Wyatt m. Dec. 14: 1731—
Wyat, son to Ben. Chamberlin b. Oct. 12: 1728—a daughter
b. Oct. 10: 1730 & d. the 19th of the same month—Benjamin
b. Dec. 27 : 1731 & d. on the 28: of the same month—

[Thus the Chamberlin record reads, being in the hand of
Mr. Bulkley.—C. M. T.]

Israel son to Ebenezer Skinner Junr. & Sarah his wife
b. Jan. 18: 1730—1—Samuell son to Nathaniel Skinner Jr
b. Sept. 11: 1735—John b. Sept. 7: 1738—Rebecca daughter to Nath. & Mary Skinner b. Dec. 3: 1730—Nathaniel b.
June 23: 1732—

Elnathan Rowley & Abigail Cone were m. Dec. 26: 1723
—Abigail b. May 7: 1725—Abigail d. Oct. 17: 1726—Jesse

b. May 8 : 1728—Abigail b. Oct. 2 : 1730—Israel b. Feb. 20 : 1732–3—Thankful b. Dec. 3 : 1735 & d. the 9 : of Dec. 1735 Abigail wife of Elnathan Rowley d. Dec. 8 : 1735—Elnathan Rowley & Lidia Wells m. Oct. 3 : 1736—Ephraim b. Oct. 17 : 1737—Thankful b.—Lydia b.

Sarah wife of Serg't Joseph Pratt died Nov. 20 : 1730

Micaiell Taintor Esq. Dyed February 19th 1730–1—Jonah son to Jonathan & Sarah Gillet d. April 10 : 1731—Aaron b. May 23 : 1732—Mary b. May 23 : 1734—The Revd Mr. John Bulkley first Minister in ye Town of Colchester departed this life in ye night following ye 9th day of June in ye year 1731,—about half an hour after one of ye clock—

Elisabeth daughter to Samuel Lewis & Mary his wife b. June 22 : 1731—Benjamin b. March 29 : 1733—Jno. b. June 16 : 1834—Samuell b. Jan. 9 : 1735–6—Abraham b. April 29 : 1738—Isaac b. Feb. 14 : 1738–9—

Young Fuller & Jerusha Bebee m. April 23 : 1730—Joshua b. Sept. 9 : 1730—

Daniel Lomis & Hannah Witherell m. Oct. 7 : 1731—Hannah b. July 15 : 1732—Mercy b. Aug. 18 : 1733—Daniel b. June 16 : 1735.

Joseph Pumery Junr & Elisabeth Randall were m. Dec. 25 : 1728—Joseph b. August 17 : 1731—Hannah b. April 28 : 1734—Abigail b. June 2 : 1736—

Prudence daughter of John & Mary Carrier b. & d. on ye 22 : March 1731—Elisha son to Serj't Isaac Bigloe b. April 14 : 1731—Abigail wife of Ensign Ephraim Wells d. Nov. 16 : 1731—Edward Fuller d. Jan 7 : 1731—David son to Edward Fuller & Elisa his wife b. Jan. 26 : 1727—Edward b. May 11 : 1730.

Eunice daughter to Benja: Aquitfield & Eunice his wife b. Feb. 26 : 1730—1.

Delight daughter to Nathl & Hannah Otis b. March 23 : 1731—Marcy b. July 3 : 1734—Delight d. July 20 : 1740—

Nathll their son d. Jan. 24: 1740–1—Hannah d. June 12: 1752 —The abovesd Nathall Otis deceased April 15: 1771 in the 81st year of his age.

Jona. son to Deac. Nathll Skinner & Mary his wife b. Aug. 15: 1721—Josiah b. April 30: 1724—Joanna b. March 19: 1727—Zerviah b. June 25: 1730—

John son to Phillip Caverly & Hannah b. Nov. 24: 1731— Phillip (son) d. June 19: 1739—John son to John & Elisabeth Douglass b. Oct. 12: 1731—Elizabeth b. Dec. 5: 1733— Daniel b. Oct. 15: 1735—

John Adams the first dyed in Colchester Nov. 22: 1732— Joseph son to Joseph Pratt Junr b. Aug. 2: 1732—Ebenezer son to John & Ann Beach b. Feb. 17: 1732-3—d. on the 5: April 1734—John son to Ebenr Skinner Jr & Sarah his wife b. Feb. 23: 1732-3—Hannah daughter to Evan & Mary Harris b. Aug. 22: 1732—James son to James Crocker b. April 20: 1732—Thankful b. Jan. 27: 1733-4.

Sarah daughter to Josiah & Grace Gates, b. Nov. 12: 1732 —Leodemiah daughter to James Newton Junr. & Susannah his wife b. May 7: 1732—Susannah b. March 15: 1735.

Elisabeth daughter to Robert & Alice Ransom b. May 1: 1729—Amy b. Aug. 2: 1732—Aaron Gillitt dyed in Boston Nov. 30: 1730—

John Chapman & Bethiah Chapman m. April 10: 1740— Bethiah b. Feb. 27: 1743—Sarah b. May 13: 1745—John b. April 6: 1747—Thomas & Jason b. Feb. 20: 1749—Rossel b. May 17: 1751—Rhoda b. Sept. 20: 1754—Rhoda d. April 20: 1756—Thomas d. Jan. 21: 1759—

Thomas son to Jabez & Ann Jones b. May 21: 1732— Jabez b. Jan. 14: 1733-4—Amos b. Jan. 2: 1734-5—Anna b. Oct. 5: 1736—Israell b. Jan. 7: 1737-8—Asa b. June 9: 1739—Hazael b. Jan. 6: 1742-3—Jehiel b. Sept. 20: 1743 —Ariel b. Sept. 28: 1745—Sarah b. Jan. 7: 1746-7—Ahijah b. July 5: 1750=

Asa son to William & Abigail Marriner b. Oct. 9 : 1732—
Jonathan son to Edward & Zerviah Bill b. May 5 : 1733—John
Quitifield & Elisabeth Kilborn m. Dec. 7 : 1733—Amasai b.
Dec. 11 : 1734—Elisabeth the wife of Charles Williams Dyed
Sept. 13 : 1725—Ruben son to John Strong & Abijah his wife
b. May 8 : 1733—

Benjamin Day & Margaret Foot m. March 6 : 1729—Ann
b. Feb. 27 : 1730—Benjamin b. Sept. 13 : 1731—Adonijah b.
July 16 : 1733—Asa b. May 16 : 1735 & d. 23 : Asa b. June
1 : 1736 & dyed 13 : Margaret b. Oct. 27 : 1737—Aaron
b. Sept. 14 : 1740—Amasai b. April 21 : 1742—Lydia b.
April 21 : 1744—Daniel b. July 21 : 1747—David b. Aug.
4 : 1749—Editha b. Jan. 5 : 1752.

William son of Jabez & Tabitha Rowley b. Oct. 15 : 1727
—Phinehas b. Oct. 7 : 1729—Lois b. Nov. 14 : 1731—Simeon
b. June 17 : 1733—Eunice b. April 3 : 1735—Nathan b. Feb.
12 : 1737—Lydia b. June 27 : 1739—Dorothy b. April 28 :
1741.

Joseph Day & Esther Hungerford m. April 1 : 1729—Ezra
b. Jan. 18 : 1730 & d. July 23 : Joseph b. May 6 : 1731—
Esther b. March 12 : 1733—Grace b. March 12 : 1736—Mary
b. July 2 : 1738—Ezra b. July 20 : 1740 & d. March 17 :
1742—Asa b. March 13 : 1743—Rachel b. Nov. 22 : 1745—
Jesse b. Jan. 16 : 1748—

Richard Quitifield & Lydia Cripen m. March 1 : 1732—
Abner b. Aug 27 : 1732—a son still-born Dec. 22 : 1733—

Jno. Carrier Junr & Rebecca Banister m. Jan. 13 : 1730–31
—Andrew b. Jan 13 : 1731–2—Mary b. Dec. 7 : 1733—Andrew d. Jan. 24 : 1736–7—Mary d. Jan. 18 : 1736–7—

Samuell Brown & Mary Dunham m. Aug. 6 : 1729—Samuell b. Aug. 17 : 1729—Abner b. March 25 : 1730—Mary b.
Feb. 13 : 1732—

Elisabeth daughter to Daniel Chamberlin b. March 18 :
1720—Esther b. Oct. 18 : 1722—Mehitabell b. Aprill 9 : 1725

—Daniel b. Nov. 2 : 1727—Richard b. July 5 : 1730—William b. March 10 : 1733—

Jabez Crippen & Thankfull Fuller m. July 9 : 1707—Susanna b. May 21 : 1708—Frances (daughter) b. June 26 : 1710—Lydia b. March 17 : 1713—Thomas b. May 15 : 1715 —Jabez b. July 14 : 1717—John b. March 20 : 1720—Mahitabell b. July 6 : 1722—Samuel b. July 7 : 1724—Joseph b. June 7 : 1726—Thankfull b. April 2 : 1728—

Cornelius Hamlin & Mary Mudge m. Dec. 5 : 1732—Cornelius b. Sept. 25 : 1733—Stephen Brainerd & Susannah Gates m. Dec. 24 : 1730—Susannah b. Sept. 24 : 1731— Elisabeth b. Dec. 17 : 1733—

Andrew Carrier Junr & Ruth Addams m. Dec. 27 : 1733— Andrew b. Nov. 9 : 1734—Ruth his wife d. Nov. 16 : 1734— Andrew Carrier & Rebecca Rockwell m. Oct. 27 : 1735—Ruth b. Aug. 14 : 1736—Joseph b. March 3 : 1738—Samuel b. Jan. 6 : 1739-40—Israell b. March 12 : 1741-2—Isaac b. April 21 : 1744—

John Ransom & Bethia Lewis m. April 6 : 1732—Robert b. April 8 : 1733—

John Gates & Sarah Fuller m. April 19 : 1722—Sarah b. Aug. 10 : 1725—John b. Aug. 19 : 1728—Nehemiah b. April 17 : 1730—Mathias b. Feb. 13 : 1733-4—Ezra b. July 20 : 1736.

John Lord & Experience Crippen were m. Dec. 26 : 1724 —Jonathan b. Oct. 3 : 1726—Timothy Carrier & Frances Crippen m. Feb. 26 : 1729-30—Elisabeth b. Jan. 18 : 1730-1— Elisabeth d. Aug. 26 : 1731—Thankfull b. Aug. 5 : 1732— Elisabeth b. Dec. 22 : 1733-4—

Hannah the wife of Mr. Benjamin Lewis died June 9 : 1732. David Day & Hannah Lewis m. Dec. 12 : 1734—

Mary, daughter to Stephen & Deborah Pain b. Dec. 29 : 1734—Deborah daughter to Ebenr. & Sarah Skinner b. Feb. 23 : 1785—Abigail daughter to Joseph & Susanna Isham b.

May 21 : 1732—Jane b. Feb. 2 : 1734—Joseph b. Oct. 15 : 1735—

Elnathan Palmiter & Elisabeth Scovele m. April 16 : 1734—Sarah b. March 18 : 1734-5—Elisabeth b. Jan. 26 : 1736-7 —Eunice b. April 11 : 1739—Elisabeth b. Dec. 11 : 1741—Irene b. May 28 : 1745—John b. Jan. 7 : 1747-8—Nathan b. March 9 : 1749-50—Charles b. Feb. 15 : 1751-2—

Daniel Chapman & Katharine Wentworth m. March 22 : 1713—Paul b. April 12 : 1714—Katharine b. Dec. 23 : 1715—Martha b. July 2 : 1717—a daughter still-born April, 1719—Sarah b. June 1 : 1720—Daniel b. April 10 : 1722—Silas b. April 8 : 1724—Elias b. Jan. 14 : 1725-6—Barabas b. March 18 : 1728—Jeremiah b. April 12 : 1733—Mercy b. April 14 : 1735—Eunice b. April 28 : 1737—Paul d. Sept. 28 : 1738—Sarah d. Dec. 22 : 1738—

John son to John Dethick b. March 10 : 1719—Elisabeth b. Dec. 17 : 1721—Susanna b. Dec. 17 : 1723—Mary b. March 10 : 1725—Sarah b. March 5 : 1727—Naomi b. May 11 : 1729—Annanias b. Dec. 24 : 1730—Hannah b. June 29 : 1733 —Ruth b. July 16 : 1734—Aaron Skinner & Eunice Taintor m. Aug 4 : 1737. Mary daughter to Ebenezer Skiner b. March 17 : 1736-7—

John Hopson & Mary Kellogg m. May 28 : 1730—John b. Nov. 5 : 1731, & d July 14 : 1732—John b. Jan. 29 : 1734—Betty b. Feb. 16 : 1735—Sarah b. Jan. 29 : 1737—Lydia b. Aug. 20 : 1739 & d. July 6 : 1740—Lydia b. Oct. 24 : 1741. Mary b. April 16 : 1745—Hannah b. Sept. 29 : 1747—Prudence b. Dec. 16 : 1750—Capt. John Hopson d. Aug. 9 : 1751 —In the 44th year of his age. March 31 : 1761 died the wife of Capt. John Hopson late deceased who after his death was joined in m. to Henry Bliss of Lebanon—Lydia their daughter d. Oct. 6 : 1761—

"Colchester Nouember 16 : 1730—then John bulkley Junr personally appeared & entered his Caution acording to ye Di-

rection of ye law of this Gouernt in pag 103: against any
Deed or euedenc of any Conueyance eighther by Josiah phelps
formerly of Colchester or by left. James haris of a Certain
tract of land Containing in quantety about Seauenty acers and
formerly Mortgaged by said phelps to John harris esqr of hartford : or any other person besids ye sd John bulkley who hath
purchased ye sd land of Roswell Saltonstall untill a legall triall
hath passed on a Deed of Releas giuen by sd phelps to sd Saltonstall hath passed to a final Issue & hath Giuen bond to me
Micaiell Taintor town Clerk—

"To All Christian people to whome these presents shall Com
greeting: Whearas the Gouerner and Company of this Colony of Conettecot in Newengland in america (By vertue of the
powers vested in them By our Late Soureign Lord king
Charles the second of Blesed memory in and by his Letters
patins under the great seal of england bareing Date the thre
& twentieth Day of Aprell in the fowrtenth year of his sd
Majests Reign did By an Instrument bareing Date the twenty-
fowrth Day of Septembr in the fowrth year of the Reign of
our soverain Lady ann: of england &c) Conuey & make ouer
unto Samull Gilbert Micaiell Taintor Samuell Northam, John
addams Joseph pumery Samuell Lomis James brown Joseph
prat & John Bulkley proprietors & freholders in the town of
Colchester & to our heigrs & assines for euer all the Land
lying in the bounds of the said town that is to say all the Land
Lying within & bounded by the folloinge boundaries : viz :
east & Northeast by a Line runing by Norwich Southwest
Bounds one mile Notherly on Norwich Line & from thenc By
a direct Line runing & falling half a mile below the midell of
the Iland in a pond Called the North pond : westerly by the
east bounds of haddam & Mideltown notherly by the north
Bownds of twenty mile Reuer Southerly by the North bownds
of the town of Lime & all the woods vnder woods vplands
areable Lands meadows pastuers ponds waters reuers fishings
10*

fowlings huntings mines Mierals quarries & prestious Stones
upon & within the sd tract of Land so butted & bownded as
aforesaid to haue & to hold the sd tract of Land with all &
singuler the heriditaments preueliges and apurtenances thareof
vnto vs the aboue mentioned Samuell Gilbert Micaiell Taintor
Samuel Northam &c & our heigrs & assines for euer to be
holden of her Majestie her heigrs & sucksesors as of her
Majesties manor of east grinwich in the County of Kent in the
Kingdom of england in fre & Comon sociage & whearas the
desire of the said gouerner & Company in the aboue mentioned
conueyanc was the settelment of a towne on said Land & the
persons hearafter mentioned (viz) William Roberds senr.
Thomas Skiner Thomas Day Joseph Chamberlin Joseph
Dewey Noah Coleman Josiah gillett ser. Isreall Wiat Charles
Williams senr. James mun John Day Joseph wright James
Taylor Richard Carier Andrew Carier Nathanll Kellog ebenezer Dibbel John Skiner Shubaiell Rowlee John brown william Shipman John Chapman ser. John waters samuel fuller
John hopson william Roberds Junr Richard Skiner Benjamin
Skiner ebenezer Skiner Josiah Strong Josiah gillet Junr Jona-
than Northam Nathll foot Josiah foot Ebenezer Colman Micai-
ell Taintor Junr. Danill Clark Junr Samll pellet Jonathan
kilburn henry tomeson John addams Junr Clement kithophell
thomas Brown John Baker Moses Rowle=haue Com & sat
Downe with vs on sd Land & made Considerable Improuements on Diuers parcels tharof=now know ye that we the
aboue mentioned Samuell Gilbert Micaiell Taintor Samuell
Northam John addams Joseph Pumery Samll Loomis James
Brown Joseph pratt & John Bulkley proprioters of the said
Land do on the Considerations aforesd Receaue the sd William
Roberds senr Thomas Skiner thomas Day with the rest of the
persons aboue named with them) as Joynt proprioters with vs
& for our selues our heigrs executors administrators & assigns
do frely Giue Grant Confirm Conuey and pass ouer unto the

said william Roberds Senr thomas Skiner thomas Day with the rest mentioned with them) them & thair heigrs for euer Such Rights in the abouesd tracts of Land as ware at thair Coming hear put in for by them (exsepting Such parcels and Rights tharof as any of them) by vertue of the pretended grants of the town) haue Disposed of (which Dispositions or Conueyances so made we do by these presents Confirm unto the persons to whom thay are Respectiuely made thair heigrs & assignes for euer) together with such pr)ueliges emunities as are hearafter mentioned & to the ondly vse bennefit & behouf of the sd persons thair & euery of thair heigrs Assigns foreuermore to haue & to hold sd parsels of Land, rights preaeliges from the day of the Date hearof foreuer) that is to Say we grant unto the aboue mentioned persons thair heigrs & assines for euer full power of acting with us in all things wharin as proprioters we may be Conserned as we ourselus haue we hauing mutuly agreed & do hearby ordaine & Determin that in all future Meetings of vs & them our & thair heigrs & assignes for euer hearafter the manegment of all afares shall be under the following Regulations (viz) that the voate of two-thirds at least of the proprioters that is to say two thirds of those who now by this Instrument are made proprioters or such as hearafter shall be) thair heigrs & assines) together with ourselus our heigrs or assigns shall be ' nessesary to the determination of any afaire in sd meetings a less Nomber shall not make a voate—2 : that none of vs our heigrs or assines or of the sd persons proprioters with vs thair heigrs that shall not haue a fiuety pownd Right (as it is Commonly Called) in the aboue mentioned tract of Land shall haue power of voating in any afaire managed in sd meetings—3 that any of vs our heigrs or assigns them or thair heigrs or assigns that Already haue or hearafter shall aduance our or thair estats and Increase our or thair Rights in Sd Land shall haue power of voating in proportion to the number of said Rights that is to say he that now has or hearafter shall haue one hundred pownd right shall haue

power of offoring two voats) he that has or shall haue a two
hundred pownd Right of fowr voats in any afaire of sd meetings & So proportionabley——in witnes whearof we the aboue
mentioned proprioters haue afixed our hands & seals this twenty
eighth Day of Aprell Anoqe Dom: 1713—Micaiell Taintor
Jno Bulkley Samll gilbert Jno addams Joseph prat Samll Northam Samll Lomis Joseph pumery—In presents of these Witneses
obadiah hosford Danll Clark senr Samuell palmer—We the
aboue mentioned persons made proprioters by the aboue Written Instrument Do hearby Signefie our aprobation of the abouementioned Rimetations for the regulation of all futuer meetings
of proprioters & Do hearby Bind our selues our heigrs &
assines to a submition to them in all futuer meetings wharin
we or thay acording to the Imuneties or preueliges in the aboue
mentioned Instrument granted may be Conserned in testemony
Wharof we haue hearto fixed our names on ye Day & year
abouementioned=William Roberds Senr thom Skiner Thom
Day Joseph chamberlin John Skiner Isreall Wiatt charles williams Jos: Dewey Jno Day Nathnll Kellogg ebenezer Dibell
Richard Carrier Shubaiell Rowlee Andrew Carier John Chapman John hopson Richd Skiner william Roberds Josiah gillet
senr Micaiell Taintor Junr Josiah gillet Junr ebenezer Skiner
thom Lomis Jonathan Kellogg Josiah foot ebenezer Colman
Jonathan Kilburn thomas Brown Samull Pellet James Newton
Josiah Strong ebenezer Kellogg Nathll foot Josiah phelps Jonathan Northam James Brown Decon Skiner Noah wels sins as
wm shipmam henry tomesons X mark Jos Wright Moses
Rowlee—

at a meeting of the proprioters of Colchester Aprell 28th
1713 the persons following haueing Com & set down with vs
& made Improuements we Do receaue them to be proprioters
of following tracts which now we grant to them (viz) to mr
James Newton yt hundred pownd Right Which he obtained of
John Chapman—To thomas Lomis that hundred pownd Right

which he bought of Daniell Cooley—To Ebenezer kellogg yt
hundred pownd Right which he purchased of Samll Waller of
N: london—To Jonathan kellog that hundred pownd Right
which he purchased of the saw-mill men—To the heigrs of Left
Noah weles Deseased yt hundred pownd Right which he took
up by vertue of a purchas made of John & Joshua more of
N. london—It was voated that mr John bulkley Joseph wright
& Micaiell Taintor shall at any time Call a meeting of the
proprioters.

at a meeting of the proprioters of Colchester July 28th:
1713—Whearas Diuers persons Do Claim Lands Within the
propriaty Granted to vs By the Gouerner & Company & from
time to time are Entering & trespasing vpon vs—it was voated
1: that Mr James Newton Samll Northam Samll Lomis Joseph Wright & Ebenezer Coleman be a Commitie for the
prosecuting & Ejecting the sd trespasers—2 that the prosecution of the sd trespasers shall be mannaged at the Comon
Charg of the proprioters & that euery one shall be Assesed
acording to his Right in the propriaty—at ye meeting aforesaid was Granted unto Ebenezer Colman fiuety acres of land
to be taken up without & Clear from the sequestrations of land
which hath bin formerly made by the towne—the Condistion
of the grant is that he the said ebenezer Coleman pay to sd
proprioters the sum of nine pounds Currant mony) at the meeting aforesd Micaiell Taintor was chosen proprioters Clerk—

at a meeting of the proprioters of Colchester october ye 23d
1717 it was voated to Grant to ye Reurt mr thatcher of milton
a quit Claim of all that part of his farm of land which lyeth
within the township of said Colchester he guieing to the said
propriaters the sum of twenty & fiue pownds: & mr bulkley
left John skiner & Micaiell Taintor are appoynted to giue sd
quit Claim in thair Name: & further it was voated that those
persons that haue taken vp land within the said farm: to take
it up elcwhare But not within any of the sequestrations of land

for town comons the persons that haue taken vp Land thare are namely Decon Samuell Lomis Benjamin addams thomas addams : Samuel brown & ebenezer Coleman & John addams which is alianated to ms elizabeth wilson of hartford—Samuell Lomis thomas addams & Samuell Brown agreed & Consented to Relinquish thar perticqler Rights of Land Layd out to them within the said Claim of mr thatchers: on the Condistions aboue mentioned & Did so Declare at the Meeting : abouementioned John addams also sent by his father to the said meeting that he agreed to the termes aboue said: benjamin addams also did the like—further it was voated that the said 25 pownds shall !be exspended towards the procuering a Bell for the town of Colchester.

Janewary 26th 1718–19—at a proprietors meeting legaly warned the proprioters voated that the present Comittie should go on in the prosecution of the action now Depending in the law against Samuell Waters of hebron: alies Colchester : and further the said Comittie namely ebenezer Colman ebenezer Skiner & nathaniell foot shall haue a further suply of mony of what is needfull in that action or any other that may happen to be of the same natuer : before another proprioters meeting (at the charg of the proprioters—at the same meeting the proprioters granted to Richard tozer seauenty acres of land : & to leftnt skiner ten acers to be taken up on the South Side of euan Joneses land : which is in Consideration that thay haue taken up Sixty acers of land in haddam bounds the which thay are exchanging with the heirs of Joseph gates— further the proprioters granted to Samuell lomis Junr liberty to mow the meadow at the deep Reuer : lying aboue the old Road to newlondon he paying to the order of the proprioters : one shilling pr load for what he doth gitt thare—

at a proprioters meeting held in Colchester Septemb 13th : 1720—they nomenated voated & apoynted Leftenant James harris ebenezer Colman & Sergt Nathanell foot a comitie to

treat & Confer with a Comittie which may be chosen by the
town or proprioters of ye town of Norwich Conserning a finall
Setlement of the bownds betwixt Norwich & Colchester: &
so to make Return to the proprioters & town of thair doings
tharein—At the meeting aforesaid the proprioters Granted to
ms foot widow fifty acers of Land to be taken up: without the
Sequestration that is to say not to be taken on any of the
Land that hath bin formerly sequestered for town Comons:
which grant is in Consideration that her Late husband Mr foot
did procuer a deed of oaneco for the township of Colchester:
& in Said deed the said Indian gaue him fifty acers for his
own perticqler use: this meeting is Adjorned till next friday
Com Seauen night—

Know All men by these presents that I Ebenezer Colemen
of Colchester In the County of hartford in his Majestis Colony
of Conettecut in Newengland Am holden & firmly do stand
bound: unto Joseph wright & Micaiell Taintor of the town
County & Colony aforesaid: who ware deputed by the proprioters of the said town of Colchester to take this bond: in
thair behalf & for the use of the said proprioters:: I say I do
hearby acknoleg my self bound unto the said Joseph Wright
& Micaiell Taintor to them or any one of them or their Attourney: or to any other person or persons who may hearafter
be deputed by the aforesaid proprioters to Receaue or Recouer
the same) in the sum of one hundred pounds Curant money:
to be paid unto the said Joseph wright & Micaiell Taintor or
thair Attourney or to him or them, who may be deputed by
said proprioters of Colchester to Receaue the same as aforesaid—to the which payment well & truly to be made: I bind
myself my heirs execoters And adminestrators firmly by these
presents: Sealed with my seal Dated the thirtenth Day of
March In the fifth year of the Reign of our Soueran—Lord
Georg: & in the year of our Lord—1719—

The Condistion of this oblygation is such that wheras at a
town meeting held in Colchester Nouembe ye 4th 1706 : the
town granted to Martin Kellogg on hundred pound Right of
Land in the town of Colchester on Condistion [that he pay to
the town fiue pounds & Com & Settell in the town) he said
Kellogg : haueing paid the fiue pounds but not Com to settell
as abouesd.) the proprioters of Colchester at thair meeting
Aprell ye 24th : 1716 granted to him Said Ebenezer Colman
that hundred pound Right : aboue mentioned, he repaying to
Said Kellogg the fiue pound & Also to bring a quit Claim
from sd kellogg of all the Right that might acrue to sd kellogg
by vertue of the Said grant : or to any of his heirs or assigns :
it is also to be understood that I the Said Colman am obliged
(hearby) to take up Said Right of Land : Within the bounds
of that which is Claimed to be the bounds of hebron : or on
the north Side or norwest sid of that Line which hebron Inhabetants pretend to be the Deuiding line betwixt hebron &
Colchester : & not to take up any part of the Said Land acrue-
ing to him by vertue of the Said Right : In any other place :
within the bounds of Colchester : : & if in Case I the said
ebenezer Colman my heirs executors or adminestrators or assigns shall well & truly perform all the aboue written premi-
eses acording to the true meaning of them : then the aboue
written obligation to be null & void & of none efect : but in
Case of failour In any part of the aboue mentioned premeses
then this obligation or within written bond to Stand in full
force Strength and vertue : to all intents & purposes of Law
whatsoeuer : & further it is to be understood that if there
should be any difeculty in the Law about the land that may be
taken up by vertue of the grant aforesaid that he said ebenezer
Colman shall defend it at his own Charg against the proprioters of hebron or the legatees of Joshua : the town nor proprioters not to be at any Charg in defending the same & if the
said ebenezer Colman Canot hold the land that he so takes up

the proprioters nor town are not obliged to make it up in any other place—In witnes wharof I haue Set to my hand & seal—Ebenezer Coleman—Signed Sealed & Deliuered in the presents of Joseph pratt Mabel Taintor her M mark—

At a meeting of the proprioters held in Colchester Septembr 23d: 1720—the proprioters granted to William brown twenty acers of land not to prejeice (prejudice, c. m. t.) any former grants to any pertcqler (particular, c. m. t.) person or to that land sequestered for town Comons—at the same meeting the proprioters granted unto ensign Nathaniell Loomis one quarter of an acer of land to bueld on: which is to be taken up Joyning to his own Land that he bought of John brown on the west side of Stebnses meadow-brook:: So as not to prejudice the high way: but if in Case he do not buld a mantion hows & settell on it: which if he doth not 'do then the grant to be void & the Land return to the town—at the same meeting was granted to Sargt prat Sergt nathaniell Kellogg nathaniel Cohoon & Joseph pratt Junr. the liberty of the Stream that runs throgh Jonathan Kellogs meadow) with about ten acers of Land: so long as thay maintain a good Saw mill on the Said brook: (or a grist mill) which if thay faile of with all Conuenient Speed to do: & and faile of maintaing a Saw-mill or Grist mill thare then the grant to be void: & the Stream & land to return to the proprioters againe—further it was granted to Mr Woodbridg liberty to take up So many acers of Land: in the undeuided Land as hadam line taks of from the land which Ms Woodbridg bought of Daniell Clark—further at the Same meeting the proprioters Chose a Comittie namely Capt wright mr Wm Worthington & Sargt Nathaniell foot to treat with the heirs of Jeremiah adams Conserning his Right of Land & make return to the proprioters—

october ye 4: 1720—At a meeting of the town & proprioters of Colchester it was voated to prefer a petistion to the generall Court to be held at Newhaven the second thirds—thirds Day.

of this Instant october Relating to a Setelment of the bounds betwixt the town of Norwich & ye town of Colchester & ebenezer Colman & Micaiell Taintor ware Apointed & Chosen to Manage thatt matter---

at a proprioters meeting held in Colchester March ye 20th: 1721---the proprioters granted to Samell Waters of hebron about twelue acers of land that the line betwixt hebron & Colchester takes into Colchester bounds---which he now hath under Improuemt---futhr granted to Noah Pumery twenty acers of land to be taken up clear from the Sequesttrations of Land Sequestered for town Comons: on Condistion that he pay to the proprioters thre pounds Curant money within one week from this meeting---

March 22d: 1721 noah pumery paid the thre pounds aboue mentioned which was deliuered to Nathaniell foot to pay to Major merit—

Aprell ye 5th: 1721 was a meeting of the proprioters of Colchester---then Capt Jos: Wright Sergt Joseph Dewey & Sergt Nathaniell foot ware Chosen a comittie to defend the sd proprioters: in an action Cominced against them by the heirs of Jeremiah addams---at the same meeting Granted to Joseph Dewey forty acers of land for the sum of sixteen pounds of Curant money forthwith to be paid to the proprioters or to thair Comittie: & sd land is not to be taken up within fiue miles distant from the meeting hows---the: proprioters meeting is adjorned until the meeting to Chous athorety—

Aprell ye 25th: 1721 was a proprioters meeting held in Colchester noah Clark petitioned for that part of the thirty acers which he bought of Cornelious Roberds: which the line betwixt Colchester & hebron Cuts of into the Colchester bounds: which was not granted) but voated that no person may take it up nor enter it on Record: until the next proprioters meeting ---further voated that Nathaniell Cahoon shall haue liberty to throw up a Corner of his lott to the Comons & to take up so

much as he throws up on the side of his lot next to the high
way : & Capt Wright & Sergt pratt are appoynted to se it
honestly don at the charg of the said Cohoon—at ye meeting
aforesd voated yt John skiner & Samuell fouller [fuller.—c. m.
t.] should take a vew of ye land within our bounds in order
to ye laying out another deuision & make Return to the proprioters—

Aprell ye 28th : 1721 was a meeting of the proprioters ye
inhabetants of Colchester it was voted to prefer a petistion to
the Generall Court in may next Relating to a Setelment of the
bounds betwixt the town of norwich & ye town of Colchester
—further voted yt the proprioters to pay the Charg thareof—
and Cap Newton Left James harris & Micaiell Taintor ware
Chosen & appoynted to manage thatt matter—at the same
meeting Capt newton & micaiell Taintor & Joseph Deuey ware
chosen to answer unto the heirs of Jeremiah adams in thair
petistion unto the generall Court in may next against the proprieters & Inhabetants of the town of Colchester—

August the 2d : 1721 was a proprioters meeting in Colchester And thay voated to sell one hundred acers of land to the
highest bidder to Raise a stock of money : for the use of the
proprioters : to pay out acording to order) it is to be understood to be without ye sequestration—further voted that leftenent Skiner shold and is hearby Impowered to sell said land &
to Giue a deed of it to the byer or biers—

August ye 24th : 1721 : was a meeting of the proprioters of
Colchester—it was voated to exchang about ten acers of land
with mr worthington at the discrestion of Leftent skiner : decon
Lomis & sergt foot & to make return to ye proprioters—further
voated yt ye abouesd comitie at ye charg of noah Clark shall
take a vew of the Land yt sd noah bought of cornelus Roberds yt falls into Colchester bounds & to sell it to sd Clark
further voated to sell ephream foot about fiue or six acers of
land which is at ye Rear of his land which he bougt of Joseph

dewey: & Joyning to John addames land he paying to the proprioters fifty shillings pr acer for so many acers as he takes—then further voated & Chose a Comitie namely mr bulkley left Wyat Sergt nathll foot Joseph chamberlin and william Roberds: to prefer a petistion to ye Generall Court in behalf of ye proprioters: against ye heirs of Jeremi adams or to procede in any other Legall way as thay shall see cause or to agree with ye sd heirs so yt ye Controuersie may be ended—further voated & appointed Lef skiner Decon Lomis & segt Nathanel foot to take a vew of ye Land which ye Contry Road taks in going thro Capt Gilberts Land & make return to ye proprioters—at the same meeting was voated to Confirm ye voat made August 2d: 1721 Relating to ye selling one hundred acers of Land & Impowering Left Skiner to sell it to ye highest bider & to pay ye money into ye tresury for ye use of ye proprioters—at the same meeting (viz) August 24: 1721 Micaiell Taintor was Chosen ye proprioters tresurer--further voated to Alter ye Rhoad yt was Laid out to lyme line: six rods wide by Left harrises Land to giue it to left harris: on Condistion yt he leaus as much In the lew of it: which is to be don at the discrestion of Left Skiner & return made of his doings tharein—

Janewary ye 17th: 172½ was a meeting of ye proprioters of Colchester then voated to quit to benjamin Gorton thair claim to fiue hundred acers of land which he bought of peter mason: within the boundaris of his Deed from sd mason which bares date Sept: ye 20: 1717: prouided that no part of it doth Infring on any former Grant or Grants of ye town or proprioters of sd Colchester: also prouided that thare be not within sd boundaries more then fiue hundred acers --further the proprioters voated to grant unto Samuell Knight so much land as the high way taks up or taks of from the front of his lot to be taken up at the west end of said lot---further voated to grant to Left harris a piece of land joyning to that farm which he bought of John

hoberd: & Joyning on the pond & brook east: on the highway
southwardly: on Consideration yt the high way goeth thro his
land: he also paying to the proprioters so much money as Left
Skiner shall Judg the sd land to be worth---further voated to
quitt Claim to Daniell palmeter the land or lotment he now
liues on :---further voated and granted to Capt. Joseph wright
the use and Improuement of the buering yard for twenty years
next Coming on Condistion that he with all Conuenient Speed
make a sufficent fence Rownd it and Clear it from bushes.---
further voated and granted to Capt wright Left Skiner Sergt
kellogg & his son sergt Andrew Carrier sergt Ephream foot
Sergt John day Sergt Jos Dewey Abraham Williams William
Worthington William Roberds & Samell kellogg fiue shillings
pr Day for thair time & expences at ye Courts in June & Nouembr last : which is forty shillings each---

March ye 27th: 1722 was a meeting of the proprioters in Colchester to Comince an action against the worshipfull mr william
pitken majr talcot & Capt Aron Cook) at ye next County
Court: for thair legall proseeding against Sundry proprioters
of Colchester in thair taking elegall fees : & the proprioters to
be at ye Charg of ye Suite---at the Same meeting : ye Reuerent
mr bulkley Left harris & Micaiel Taintor ware Chosen a Comi-
itie to Attend the Comitie appointed by ye Generll Court: to
settell the bounds betwixt norwich & Colchester further Granted
to mr. bulkley thirty acers of Land: to be taken up without
the Sequestration---further at the same meeting Ephream foot
was exsepted a proprioter: for a fifty pound Right in the pro-
priotie of Colchester in all after deuisions of land he paying to
ye proprioters the Sum of fowr pounds money---

At a proprioters meeting Aprell 24th: 1722 it was voated
and Granted to Left John holmes that thirty acers of land
which was formerly designed to be Confirmed unto thomas
Grstin---for the Consideration of twenty pounds money—at the
same meeting it was Granted to Left holms aforesd that he

shall haue ye Rear of his lot that he now lius on : to be ex-
tended to the hill or Ledg of Rocks in Consideration of the
high way that is Laid out thro his land—at ye same meeting
ensign foot & sergt kellogg ware appointed in behalf of the
proprioters to Recon with ebenezer Colman—

June ye 4th: 1722 was a meeting of the proprioters: thay
then Chose a Comittie namely Left Wyat Ensign foot &
Micaell Taintor to Recon & pay to the persons that haue bin
Conserned at the Court by a voat of the proprioters: in the
Controuersie with ye heirs of Jeremi addams & other Cases in
Court Arising tharefrom : & to pay out to each one his due---
at the meeting aforesd it was voated to Sell Josiah Gates fifty
acers of Land for twenty fiue pounds and that on the payment
tharof the abouesd Comittie to Giue him a Deed of it in the
name & behalf of the proprioters—

at a proprioters meeting in Colchester Nouembr 5th: 1723
—voated that the reuerend mr bulkley & ensign foot shold defend the proprioters of Colchester in the action Cominced
against them by ebenezer Coalman to be tried at hartford—

Janewary the 14th : 172¾ was a Legall meeting of the proprioters of Colchester & it was voated to Confirm the voat
wherin it was granted unto Josiah gates & Confirm unto Josiah
gates the sd Land : which was granted at a meeting Nouember
5th: 1723 that not being a full meeting : further voated that
nothing shall be voated after the Sun is set in any meeting of
the proprioters---the meeting is adjorned untill wednsday Com
Seauen-night at nine of the clock in the morning—

Janewary the 22: thare being but a few appearing acording
to the aboue ajornment : the meeting is furder ajorned untill
the second munday of februwary next ensueing this Date—

at a Legall meeting of the proprioters of Colchester begun
febry ye 10th : 1724 & Continued till ye end of ye 11th Day
of ye same---wharas at ye meeting abouesd (viz) Janey 14th :

172¾ Micaiell Taiutor was Chosen proprioters Clerk, he is now Sworn to yt office acording to Law—Voated that Whareas thare has arisen a Controuersie betwen the proprioters & Claimers of Land in ye town of Colchester on ye one part and thomas kimberly of glosenbery on the other part Respecting a grant made by ye sd proprioters to ye sd thomas kimberly at their meeting March 12th: An; Dom: 1715--16 of thre hundred acers of Land near ye Great Pond in Colchester: on the Rhoad to Glasenbery & was surueyed & layd out to him thare by ye town measurer: the sd proprioters being now mett Willing to adjust & Isue ye Controversie in ye most peacable and Louing manner yt may be) haue Giuen & do now Giue unto the sd thomas Kimberly one hundred and fifty acers of Land to be taken vp within sd tract so surueyed and measured & upon one side tharof to be to him the sd thomas kimberly his heirs & assigns foreuer to be laid out by ye town surueyer, prouided ye sd Thomas Kimberly shall by an Instrument Duly Executed Relinquish & quitt his Claim to ye Remainder of ye sd thre hundred acers to ye sd proprioters thair heirs & assigns foreuer=Which Instrument the said Thomas kimberly hath now Executed--further at the meting mentioned on the other side it was voated that All the Lands not Already Laid out on ye nor west End of the town Lying betwene ye Sequestration made by the proprioters at their meeting---on ye east & west sides of ye town quiite vp to Joseph Deweys mill Brook & Jeremis Reuer be Sequestred to the town their heirs & sucksesors for euer Town Comons for euer---it was Also voated yt Leftt Wyat Left Skiner & Sergt prat shall Be a Comittie to set out ye bounds of the seques-trations made by the proprioters on the east west north & south sids of the town—At their meeting Sept 30th; 1715: & yt they make Return of thair doings tharein to ye proprioters---further it was voated to Choose a Comit-tie to measure ye Land yt ye Stubnese Claimed in ye bounds of Colchester: & make return to the next meeting of the proprioters---and also yt ye persons Claiming under sd Stubinses be notefied to be present at ye Suruey of sd Lands---and Left Skiner ensn foot & Ebenezer Colman ware Chosen a Comittie to Do yt matter: & also to notefie ye persons Conserned as aboue sd---further at the same meeting Granted to John Taylor twenty acers of Land which he bought of Capt peter mason as it Lyeth Joyning on the west side of land which he bought of Daniell Rogers---the proprioters meeting is adjorned untill the last munday of march next at ten of the clock—

Whearas thare haueing arisen a Controversie betwene the proprioters & Claimers of Land in ye town of Colchester in ye County of hartford in ye Colony of Conettecut in New england on ye one part, & thomas kimberly of glosenbery within ye sd County on the other part Respecting a grant made by ye said proprioters to the said tho: Kimberly at their meeting March 12th: 1715--16 of thre hundred acers of Land near ye Great Pond in said Colchester on ye Rhoad to Glasenbery & surueyed and laid out to him thare by the town mesurer & whearas the said proprioters at thair meeting in Colchester aforsd febrewary 11th: 1723--24, to ye intent yt thay may Com to a Loueing & peacable adjustment & Isue of the Said Coytrouersie: did then giue & grant to ye Said thomas kimberly one hundred & fifty acers of Land to be taken vp within the sd tract, prouided ye said thomas kimberly shall by an Instrument Duly excuted Relinquish & quitt his Claim to the Remander of the Said thre hundred acers to ye sd proprioters as Referanc to ye grant aforesd of februwary 11th: aforesd being had may more fully apeare: know all men therefore by these presents that I ye sd thomas kimberly Do for myself my heirs executors & adminestrators fuly frely Clearly & absolutely Relinquish & quitt all my Right & Claim to & in

ye aforesd Remainder or Resedue of ye said thre hundred acers
of Land unto ye said proprioters to haue & to hold, the aboue
premeses unto them ye said Proprioters & to their heirs &
assigns for euer, & I ye said thomas kimberly Do hearby for
myself my heirs executors & adminestrators : Couenant promice
& grant to & with the said proprioters & their heirs & assigns
in ye folowing maner yt is to say thair heirs & assigns shall or
lawfully may from and after ye Day of ye Date hearof : & at all
times hearafter peacably & quietly haue hold use ocupie possess
& Injoy ye afore promised & Released premeses with ye apurtenances profits & aduantages thearof : to thair onely & sole Bene-
fitt & behouff without ye Lawfull lett suits molestation Contre-
diction euiction ejection or disturbanc from me ye said thomas
kimberly my heirs executors or adminestrators or any other
person or persons whatsoeuer Lawfully Claiming or to Claim
from by or under me : In witnes whearof I haue set to my
hand & seal thes 11th : Day of febrewary Anaqe Dom :
1723--24—   THOMAS KIMBERLY—

  Signed Sealed & Deliuered In presence of vs
              Daniell Chamberlin John Taylor—

Colchester februwary ye 11th : 1723-4, then thomas kimberly
the aboue subscriber & within Granter personally appeared before me the underwrighter & acknoleged the aboue & within
written Instrument to be his free act & Deed—
        MICAIELL TAINTOR Justice of ye Peace—

Aprell 16th : 1724 then bounded out the first sequestration
by vs (" Isreall Wyat ") Joseph prat & John Skiner a Comittie
Chosen for that work : begining at the Rear of maddam willsons home lot then Runing easterly by browns Path to a black
oak tre standing on the south side of the path a heap of stones
about it : then Runeth southerly by the front of Daniell Clarks

Josiah foots Nathll foots & ye Rest of them Deuisions to ye Rhoad to N. london: then westerly by long-meadow & the swomp that belongs to ye welses & then by Josiah phelpses meadow & then by phelpses Land to the Road to Lyime: from thenc by the north end of Richard Churches Land & then Runing by the north end of sergt Chapmans farm he now liues vpon & then Runing by the north line of that tract of land which was sergt Rowlees first deuision then a streight line to the south end of kilburns fall swamp: then by that Land west to Decon Lomise first deuision : then Notherly by the front of that Deuision & John skin r; first Deuision to the Rhoad to modus: all the land within these bounds exsepting such land as is legally laid out is to be sequestered town Comons for euer : Voated & exsepted by the proprioters at their meeting June ye 9th=1724—

At ye meeting aforsd (Sept : ye 14 : 1730) it was voated yt Capt. wright & Decon skiner be a Comitie with power to Inquier into ye quantety of land sold by Robert Stapels to Cololl Brown & make sale of ye same to Raise money for ye proprioters present nesesety—

March 19th : 1724 : Then bounded out the sequestration of land on the east side of ye town by us Isreall Wyat Joseph pratt & John Skiner a Comittie appoynted for yt work) which is don as followeth,) begining first at a black oak tre marked stons about it by the norwest part of the north meadow : from thenc Runeth North & be west half a mile on the westely side of the hill : to a peperag tree marked stones about it in the southerly part of a bogee & bushee pice of meadow : from thenc east across the hill first to a white oak tre markt stons about it on the brow of the hill: from thenc to a Chesnut tree markt stons about it on the top of the hill thenc to a black oak staddell markt stons about it by a ledg of Rocks; from thenc to a popel stadel markt stons about it by a pople swomp which is ye noreast Corner from thenc south & be east or near thare about: to a white oak tree stones about it which is ye norwest Corner bounds of Joseph prats farm which was formerly Joseph Deweys then by that farm to ye souwest Corner bounds: from thenc by a litell swamp of Joseph prats & then by the brook that Runs out of sd swomp to Capt Wrights pond then by Capt wrights to ye brook that empties itself out of sd pond which is Called stony brook from thenc by the brook to Jonathan kellogs meadow: so by ye brook to labanon old path whare it Croseth the sd brook: from thenc westerly by the Rhoad to a black oak tre marked stons about it by ye path: from thenc by ye Rhoad which Rhoad Coms by Jonathan Kelloggs hows: & so Coms into the town Street by Decon Lomises hows:—

March 22: 1724 then bounded out the sequestred land on the West side of the town and other land which is not yet sequestered begining at ebenezer kellogs southwest Corner bounds of his land that his hows stands on from thenc westerly by Moodus Rhoad to sd kellogs south west Corner bounds a heap of stons: from thenc westerly to Richard Carriers hows from thenc by the Rhoad to a walnut tree stons about it which is George Sexstons Corner: then by Sexstons land & Richard Cariers land to pine swomp: then notherly to north end of sd swomp: then Runing by the brook till in Coms to a place whare it emptieth itself into Jeremiahs Reuer: then Runing by the reuer till it Coms to a place whare Joseph Deweys mill brook emptieth itself into Jeremis Reuer then Runing by sd brook till it Coms whare it Runs out of the north meadow then on the westerly side of sd north meadow to the black oak tre which is ye first bounds mentioned in the sequestered Land on the east side of the town which boundaries take In all the land within these bounds to be sequestered Comons for euer exsepting such as is legally Layd out:—

This Return of the Comittie was exsepted of by the proprioters and voated at their meeting aforesd : viz : March 30th : 1724"—

At the Meeting aforesaid (date gone) the proprioters granted mr thomas kimberly his heigrs & asigns for euer thre hundred acres of land which land was taken up By his father eliezer kimberly by vertue of a Court Grant & other Purchas & Now falls within Colchester township & that Colchester town surueyer of land shall on the charg of said kimberly make a new suruey of sd thre hundred acres of Land—further at the same meeting it was Granted to thomas Dickerson that part of his farm that he hath taken up By vertue of Court grants: we say we Do grant that part to him of said farm that falls in Colchester township—further at the same meeting wharas seuerall of the Comitie Chosen at a proprioters meeting July 28th: 1713 to prosecute trespasers on our land Desired a relese from yt work it was voated To Releas all of them Exsepting Ebenezer Coleman & further Ebenezer Skiner & Nathaniell foot with sd Coleman are now voated and apointed to be a Comitie to manage that afaire acording as is exprest in that act made at said meeting—

December ye 3d : 1730—Receaued of Leftenant Skiner for ye use of ye proprioters the sum of nine pounds thirteen shillings which was for land sold to Joseph pepoon—

Janewary ye 2d—1730: 31—more Receaued of left Skiner fowr pounds seauen shillings—paid out of the abouesd sum to left Skiner by order of ye Comitie the sum of thre pounds thre shillings—paid out the remainder of the nine pounds 13s to mr John bulkley Junr which is 6lb 10s—

(The following is Mr. Taintor's last entry in the public Records, it being one week before his decease.—C. M. T.)

" february ye 12 : 1730--31—Receaued of left Skiner the sum of six pounds which he had of Decon stephen brainerd for 4 acers & 48 Rods of land—

at a meeting of ye fremen the last tuesday of aprell : 1724 than a proprioters meeting was apoynted to be held on the second tuesday of June next

June the 9th 1724 was a proprieters meeting held in Colchester—it was voated that such Gentlemen at N: london or elsewhare thair heirs or asigns as claim under the Stubinses that haue not as yet had thair home lots wth thair first & second Deusion shall haue liberty forthwith to lay out said Deuisions out of the sequestration : & yt as for their third Deuision thay with such as haue had thair first & second Deuision already shall draw for it with ye rest of ye proprioters of the town when thay shall draw for the next Deuision— Voated at the meeting aforsd yt whearas the proprioters of the town are already Indebted & further charg is likely sudenly to arise on them) that money for defraying such charges shall be Raised by thair sale of lands & yt Capt wright & left skiner shall be a Comitie to dispose & giue Conueyences of such parsels of Land as by them shall be thought meet to be sold : & to receaue the money for such Lands & make disburstments of it to perticqler persons to whome it shall appear to them acting with micaill taynter Left wyat & ensign foot : who with them are to adjust the acounts of the propriatey whare the proprioters are Indebted—

Aprell 16th : 1724 then bounded out the first sequestration : by us Isreall Wyat Joseph prat & John Skiner a Comittie Chosen for that work : begining at the rear of maddam Willsons home lot then Runing easterly by browns path to a black oak tree * * * * *

Septembr 30th : 1724 : was a proprioters meeting held in Colchester—it was voated (unanemusly : that for the futuer at the meetings of the proprioters : the Major part of the sd proprioters then present : shall make a voat in any matter or thing : & that is acording to ye Regulation of ye Law in yt behalf—further voated to Desire the reuerend Mr Bulkley

(yt if thare should be ocasion: that he would go to the generall Court in october next to act & Do for us in the matter of
the bounds betwixt hebron & Colchester—the meeting is Adjorned untill the second munday of october next—

at a Legall meeting of the proprioters of the undeuided
Lands in ye town of Colchester october ye 12th: 1724: the
Reuerend mr bulkley moderator: Joseph wright Chosen pro
temporary Clerk: at ye meeting aforesd it was voated that
thare should be as soon as may be Conueniant a Deuision of
Lands Laid out in the undeuided Lands: (viz) one hundred
acers to a two hundred pound Right & fifty acers to a one
hundred pound Right & so proportionably to a greater & leser
Right: & it was further voated & agreed that lots shall now
be drawn for ye Deuisions aforesd which ye proprioters proseed & an acount tharof taken with the number to each persons name anexted & it was agreed yt persons should take
thair turns to haue thair Deuisions Laid out acording to the
number thay Draw begining at ye first & so on & it was further voated & agreed that an estemation shall be made in Laying out ye Deuisions: of each mans Deuision & ye quantety
of it encreased or Demineshed acording to ye qualety of it &
yt Left Wyat & Samull fuller shall be a Comittie to attend
Left Skiner in the suruey & to make sd estemation & yt In
Case whare thay Cant agree Left Skiner to he umpier) But
it is to be understood that wheneuer any person is willing to
refer ye estemation of his Land to Left Skiner alone he shall
haue liberty so to doe & it was further voated that the first
four in number shall haue liberty to haue thair Deuisions laid
out in the last week of this Instant october sucksesiuely as
thay fall & so ye next fowr in ye next week following & so in
that maner untill all be fineshed & in Case any neglect to lay
his land out in his appoynted time ye next in number may lay
out before him—At the meeting aforsd it was voated & Granted

that ye Reuerend Mr: Bulkley shall haue an equivolent for what he has thrown of from the Rear of his home lott—

Aprell ye 11th: 1726 was a legall proprioters meeting held in Colchester: the Reuerant mr bulkley ensigne foot Corporall Roberds: Capt wright Left skiner & Micaiell Taintor ware Chosen a Comittie to mannag all our Conserns in the Law: whatsoeuer: as thare may be ocasion—further voated & granted to Left holmes one acer of Land & fifteen Rods Joyning to his own Land on Condistion that he discharg the proprioters from any demands of money that is now due to him from the proprioters—

Aprell ye 25th: 1727: was a proprioters meeting in Colchester: then granted to nathaniel foot: all the Right of land which the town of Colchester had of William Shipman Late of hebron deceased) in ye township of hebron which was his Legate Right in sd township: which sd Shipman gaue to ye proprioters of Colchester) in Consideration of a two hundred pound Right yt ye proprioters of Colchester granted to said Shipman—further voated & sequestered to be town Comons for euer about two acers of Land: which Land lyeth Joyning to thomas Lomises land on ye Easterly side of the Rhoad before sd lomises hows: for ye Conueniency of water: to begin at ye southerly Corner of Samuel Lomises land & So to run a South line till it Comprehends two acers—further at the meeting aforesd granted to Jonathan kilburn that hundred acers of Land which he formerly purchased of Samuel pellet at a place called paugwonk: & is now granted to him sd kilburn for a further Confirmation of his former purchas of sd pellet'—

at a legall proprioters meeting holden in Colchester Janey 16th: 1727: at ye meeting &c whearas Joshua wheler of Newlondon was a proprioter of land in Colchester and Complains he hath not had his 3d: deuision laid out (yet) it is voated yt a Comitie shall be Chosen to lay out to sd wheler or his order his 3d deuision or any part of it & yt ensn foot & decon Tain-

tor be ye Comittie to lay out sd land—wharas at a meeting of
ye proprioters octob 23: 1717 it was voated yt such persons
as had taken up lands within ye Claim of ye Reuert mr thacher
of milton should haue libertie on thair quiting sd lands to take
up elswhere in ye undiuided land of ye town & wharas ms eli:
willson of hartford in Right of ebenzr Colman of this town
had lands within sd Claim which lands she has not to this day
seen Cause to throw up & take up elswhare in Consideration
yt ye proprioters (had released?) to him more land then thay
ware knowing to: it is now voated ye sd land shall not be
taken up elswhare in ye undeuided lands of ye town—it was
further voated yt ye proprioters shall bare ye nesesary Charg
yt ebenezer Colman & John strong shall be at in defending:
against a Lawfull Comittie against them by the proprioters of
ye fiue miles in labanon—

the prayer of Noah Coleman to ye proprioters of Colchester humbly showeth that I haueing 93 acers of land on ye
east bounds of ye town of sd Colchester: on which I would
settell if I Could obtain an open way thareto: which now it
hath not therefore I would humbly pray the gentlemen proprioters of Colchester yt thay would appoint & Impower
Mr John Skiner & mr Josiah strong to be a Comittie to
agre & exchang land with Left Wyat: acer for acer or
sumthing more if thay sd Comittie think meet: takeing from
Mr Wyats Deuision which lyeth on ye soueast of sd Colmans
Deuision & off from ye west end of sd Deuision for a high
way: & to make up to mr Wyat so much land in quantetie &
qualety on or Joyning to sd Wyats Deuision: on ye east Joyning to labanon bounds or elswhare whare it may be found Joyning unto his sd Wyats land: all the Charg of men & action to
be defrayd by me Noah Coleman Jeney 16th: 172¼ Voated—
by ye proprioters at ye meeting aforesd—this return exsepted
by sd Noah Colman & Clerk noah wells heirs to left Isreall
Wyat do agree & in euedence thareto do set to thair hands
Noah Wells Noah Coleman—

february ye 10th: 1728–9 was a proprioters meeting held
in Colchester at which meeting the proprioters being Informed
yt sundry persons of hebron & other places) haue or do pre-
sume to make enteranc upon our lands Joyning to midletown
or adjacent) both Deuided or undeuided) therfore at the meeting aforesd ye Reuerent Mr. John bulkley Capt Joseph wright
& lef: Jno skiner ware Chosen a Committee to prosecute any
person or persons yt shall or may at any time ventuer to tres-
pas on any of our Lands aforesaid—

at a meeting of ye proprioters held in Colchester March ye
5th: 1729 it was voated yt mr bulkley Capt wright Decon Jno
Skiner or such of them as thay shall agre shall with all Conuienient Speed go to Midletown & Inquier into ye tru State of
ye origenal Grant perticqlerly as to ye eastward abutments of
it: as Also what Lands ye line lately run & agreed upon by
Comittis apointed by them & vs (may Includ in ye township
of Mideltown ouer & aboue thair sd origenal & yt thay finally
agre with mideltown: & to preuent any futuer Controversy yt
may arise Respecting sd line) shall in our behalf Giue to mideltown a Deed of sale of what part of our Lands thay may
find Included by sd line, thay shall se Caues prouided thay
will Com in & be a part with vs in ye Charg yt shall arise in
ye suit at Law now to be Cominced, by said Comittie against
som of hebron with others who haue Inuaded that quarter) it
was voated also at ye same meeting yt mr benjamin Lewes &
ensign Nathaniel foot be added to ye Comitie abousd to act in
Concert with them in ye afairs Comitted to them—

June ye 17th: 1729 was a proprioters meeting held in Colchester: it was voated yt whareas Capt wright & left Skiner
ware formerly Impowered to sell som of ye proprioters Land
in Colchester: & thay haueing lately sold to Aaron Gillet one
hundred acers as may apear by a Deed giuen by them to sd
Gillet bareing Date ye 26th: Day of May 1729 (we do now
Ratefie & Confirm the land so sold unto the sd Gillet & to his

12*

heirs & assigns foreuer—at ye same meeting ye Rered mr
bulkley ensn Nathaniell foot Decon John skiner mr benjamin
Lewes & sergt william Roberds ware Chosen a Comitie with
power to Do whatsoeuer shall be further nesesary for the de-
fenc of the northwestern quarter of the propriaty now Inuaded
by som of hebron & others—further Micaiell Taintor was
Chosen tresurer to receaue and pay out the mony of the proprioters as he shall receaue order from a Comittie to be appointed to audit & adjust ye acounts of ye propriaty—further
at ye meeting aforesd Joseph Chamberlin sergt John Day &
Daniell Clark ware Chosen a Comitte to audit & adjust ye
acoumbts of the propriaty & signe orders to ye tresurer to
make payment of its Just Debts, & further are Impowered to
make & sue out ye Demands of ye propriety on any persons
whatsoeuer & the meeting is adjorned untill tomorowe at one
of ye Clock in ye afternoone—

the proprioters mett according to adjornment & adjorned the
meeting untill the 3d Day of July at one of ye Clock—

the proprioters met acording to adjornment ye 3d Day of
July 1729—it being Reported by sundry persons present at
this meeting yt seuerall persons in fencing in thayr Deuisions
haue incroacht upon the Commons & Inclosed Considerably
beyond thair grants & abutments & yt others haue disposed. of
ye proprioters Lands) it was voated yt Decon skiner ensign
foot & sergt Roberds be a Comitie with power at ye Charg of
ye proprioters to Inquier into ye abouementioned wrongs & to
take such measures for rectefying of them as ye law directs
to—

September ye 1t 1729 was a proprioters meeting held in
Colchester—the matter of John tomson refered untill the next
proprioters meeting also the matter signefied by lefent harrises
Lotmt also Refered till the next meeting.

At a meeting of ye proprioters in Colchester by adjornment
Septembr 9th: 1729 it was voated to acquit Leftenant harris

of any demand of yt fifty acers of Land which he sd harris
hath Laid out at paugwonk in Right of James brown late of
Colchester on Consideration yt he pay to ye proprioters the
sum of fifty pounds for which he hath giuen bond to pay to
Micaiell for ye use of ye proprioters.

May 11th : 1730 was a proprioters meeting held in Colchester—a Comitie was Chosen to lay out highways namely Decon
skiner sergt kellogg & ebenezer Dible who are as soone as may
be to Do that which is needefull in yt matter & make return
to ye proprioters—further at ye same meeting it was voted yt
wharas ensign foot John bulkley Junr and William Roberd
ware Chosen a Comitie with power to treat with a Comitie
from Labanon respecting such Controuersis as are now depending in ye Law or otherwise betwene ye proprioters of this town
& the proprioters of labanon & finally to determin ye same as
also to agre upon a line betwene us & them & whearas ye sd
Comittis haue on ye eighth Day of this Instant may treated &
Com to an agrement with a Comitie from labanon on the
premeses & now make Report tharof to this meeting it is now
voated yt ye sd agrement be now exsepted & in all ye parts
tharof be Complyed with & yt it be entered on ye proprioters
records—further at ye same meeting ye proprioters voated yt
a person such as the Commitie shall Determin shall at ye Charg
of ye proprioters as soon as may be, go to one mr latrop in ye
prouince of ye Masachusets & treat with him about an exchang of such lands of his as by a late agrement with labanon
may—

September ye 14 : 1730 was a proprioters meeting held at
Colchester—it was voated to sell Land to Raise money) to the
value of fifty pounds for the use of the proprioters & lefent
skiner is hearby Impowered to sell so much land as to Raise the
sd money as aforesd—Sergt Nathaniell kellogg enters his protest against ye aboue written voat—further at ye same meeting
Left. Skiner ensign foot & william Roberts ware Chosen a

Comitie to search the bounds of fitches farm at Deep brook—the meeting is adjorned till to morow after ye freemens meeting.

the proprioters met acording to adjornment—at ye meeting aforesd it was voated yt Capt. wright and sergt kellogg be a Comitie with power to Do wt may be thought most proper for ye atainment of a certain tract of land belonging to Colll Isaac latrop of plimoth &c—but with yt limetation yt before they Conclude anything with relation to yt matter thay make Report of their proseedings to ye proprioters of ye town & take thair opinion & aduice tharein—further at ye same meeting it was voated yt ye Reuerend mr bulkley Capt wright Decon skiner ensign foot & John bulkley Junr: be a Comitie to aduise upon Draw up & offer what they may think proper: to ye Asembly in october next for ye attainment of (satisfaction?—c. м. т.) Respecting the Dificultis we haue bin at & are like to be under on our northern bounds—

March ye 20th: 1728: was a proprioters meeting in Colchester—whareas left harris hath taken up fifty acers of land which he hath no right to therefore the proprioters chose Capt wright left Skiner & Ensign foot Comittie to treat with sd left harris & agree with Left haris Relating to yt matter. at the meeting aforesd Left Skiner & ensign foot ware Chosen a Comitie to mesuer the land yt James brown liued on & sold: & also on ye desire of John brown to sarch ye Record Conserning his Right of land in Colchester—at ye meeting aforesd it was voated yt Daiell burge shall haue yt 60 acers of land he now lius upon that is to say ye proprioters quit thair Clain to the sd sixty acers of Land—further voated that If the Comittie Chosen by the town to Clear of Incomberances on highways or Comons Shall se ocasion to Remoue sergnt Joseph deweys fence he has set up on ye Comons or highways or undeuided lands: & enter into ye Law & prosecute yt matter threw) the proprioters will be at ye Charg of said prosecution—

whareas Joshua wheler of Newlondon was a propriotor to land in Colchester & hath not (yet his third deuision Laid out

to him whare upon at a proprioters meeting in Colchester Janewary 16th : 1728 the proprioters Chose decon taintor & Nathll
foot to lay out for aron Gillet (on sd Whelers Right) one hundred acers of Land which was sd whelers 3d deuision) which
sd aaron Gillet hath bought as Appears by Deed—In pursue-
ance we the subscribers did on ye 15th day of march A. Dom
1728) lay out to ye sd Aaron Gillet on sd whelers Right) as
followeth first fifty acers of land Lying on ye west side of pine
Swomp brook   *   *   *   *   *   Laid out ye day & year
abouementioned.   Micaiell Taintor Nathll foot Comitie Chosen
for that work—Recorded March 24th : 1728.

at a meeting held Janewary the 15th : 1710–11 Daniell
Clark payed the proprioters forty shillings : to be Disposed of
for the ejecting of any person or persons that shall or may
make enteranc upon our Right without the Consent of the proprioters : & also to pay further to that purpose a share with
the Rest of the proprioters as ocasion *shall* be) equall with
those that pay for a two hundred pound right—

At a proprioters meeting held in Colchester June 28th :
1715—it was unanamously voated to lay out a fowrth Deuision
of Land : of fifty acres to a hundred pound Right as it is
Caled : & to be Drawn for and Laid out in the same manner
as hath bin formerly practised : also he that Draws the figur 1 :
to haue the first choice that is to say to take up his proportion
the first : and so sucksessiuely & that he that doth not take
up or Lay out his deuision within six month from & after the
Date abouesd : shall haue no preuelig by the number of his
Draught : but then euery one shall haue liberty Alike—at the
meeting aforesaid the proprioters appoynted John skiner to
make som addistion unto that hundred acres of Land laid out
to Joshua hemsted at a place Called paugwonk : for the conuenienc of bringing his Land to the Rhoad & sd hemsted is to
Leaue out so much as is added there : out of his Deuision of
Land on the east side of the town plot which lyeth at or near

labanon old Rhoad : further the proprioters voated & apoynted
John skiner to Joyne with Jonathan hill Joshua hemsted Christopher Stebins or any other Conserned in that tract of Land
which is Called Stebenses & resign sd Land to the town of
Colchester—

At A meeting of the proprioters of Colchester held
Septembr ye 30th : 1715. the proprioters granted to william Robords Juner ten acres of Land joyning to his home
lott : & his other Deuision Land : on condistion that Joseph
Dewey relinquish & giue up to the Comons that seuen acres of
Land at the rear of John Jonsons home lot : which If said
Dewey Doth : then sd Dewey shall also haue Liberty to take
up seauen acres in lew of it : & to take it not within two miles
of the *town platt* & Micaiell Taintor senr is hearby Impowered
to take a Deed of the sd Land of the sd Dewey in behalf of
the proprioters to be town Comons for euer : at ye meeting
aforesaid the proprioters Reserue that Land from mr eliots
third Deuision Land to midelltowne Bounds whare it Crosses
Samon Reuer : & so from mr eliots Land to Richard Cariers
Deuision : that no person shall take up any Land thare untill
our Comitie have Don with easthaddam Comitie as to exchang
of Land : at the meeting aforesaid the proprioters Declared by
a voate that thay did Relinquish stubinses titell of Land, that is
to say all yt part of it that lyeth in east haddam Bounds :—at
the same meeting the proprioters voated to Confirm that sequestration of Land made By the towne Jenewary the 24th :
1705 : we say we do now giue it vp to be town Comons for
euer as it is thare prescribed : exsepting what is Granted, &
layd out to ephream foot & others that haue Already Layd out
land Regulerly within sd Bounds : or exchanges of Land
already made & not yet Layd out : further the proprioters
voated to sequester for towne Comons for euer : all the Land
on the east side of the town : that is not Already Layd out that
is to say to Begin at the upper or north end of the north

meadow & from that to run on the west side of the hill half a
(mile ?) thenc it runs acros the hill easterly to a poppell swomp.

At a meeting of the proprioters of Colchester Aprell the
30th :—the proprioters voated that whare it hath hapened that
in the Runing of the bounds betwene our Neighbouring towns
& us any part of any perticqler Deuision be Cut of or Left
out from our town bounds : the surueyer is hearby Impowered
to Lay out so much Land to the persons so sufering as is taken
of by said lines : & to be taken Joyning to the said Deuision
if thare be Room : the like may be Don by any perticqler persons that Interfear : by thair Deuision in laping one Deuision
on another in former layings out :

At a meeting of the proprioters of Colchester June ye 12th :
1716—the proprioters voated to make void the Return of the
suruey of land for Major John Leuinston Dated Janewary the
10th : 1709–10 it being laid out By John Skiner & Samll pellett—thay haueing layd out one hundred acers more then the
Grant was :

at a proprioters meeting held in Colchester Nouember the
3d : 17— the proprioters voated to Confirm the grant formerly
granted to Major John Leueston of two hundred acers of land
by the town : to be taken up acording to the said grant : &
not to Infring upon any other former grants or former layings
out : granted by the town or proprioters—at the meeting aforesaid the proprioters voated yt the land Lately Recouered in the
law of Samuell waters alies Coleman of hebron shall not be
taken up by any person : but be disposed of by the proprioters
& no other way—

June 12th : 1716 was a meeting of the proprioters of Colchester : Samuell Northam & Capt Gilbert ware Chosen a
Commitie to Inquier & git the best Information thay Can by
taking a vew of the Land which mr thatcher Claims within the
township of Colchester & make Returne to the next proprioters meeting—further the proprioters passed a voat that the

seting up in wrighting on ye meeting hous dore the time when thare is a proprioters meeting apoynted at least ten days before the time apoynted: shall be a sufficient warning for such meeting—

Wharas sundry persons haue thro a misunderstanding of the sequestration of town Comons made September 30th: 1715: laid out & Caused to be Recorded sundry tracts of land as fourth Deuision within sd sequestration: we sd proprioters Do now Declare By a voate that all such layings out & records to Be Elegall: & that the persons that haue so taken up land shall haue libertie to take up thair Deuisions elce whare—At the same meeting the proprioters did further sequester on the west side of the town begining at Richard Carriers hows & to Run by moudus road till it Coms to saxtons Land: thenc to run west till it Coms to ye pine swomp: then to run on the east side of sd pine swomp till it Com to Jeremis Reuer: exsepting what is Already Layd out: all the Remander to Be & Remaine to Be town Comons for euer—

The following is taken from the Watrous Copy of the 1st Book of Colchester Town Records—viz:

"Att a Town meeting held at Colchester Jan. 11: 1703, granted unto Samuel Loomis & John Skiner their first Devision of land on the Hill where they have broken up—Nextly granted to Ebenezer Dibble his first Division of upland on the West hill where he hath broke up—Further granted Charles Williamses Division shall ly on the south side of Samuel Loomis:s Division—Next granted John Adams:s Division * * * * Next granted to William Shipman a home lott on the south side of John Hopsons home lott on condition that he come off the Hill and live on it—

Further it was voted that every man shall be obloyged and absolutely bound to cut down all the under Brush half the way

across the Street against his home-lott—and every one that
shall fall eney tree in the Street shall clear it out of the Street
within one month after he hath fallen it & if he doth not he
shall pay five shillings to him that shall clear it out from the
Street—

At a Town meeting February 3rd 1703 Granted to Andrew
Carrier the swamp * * * Nextly granted to John Skinner the swamp lying at the northwest end of Long-meadow—
Nextly granted to Josiah Gillet & his sone Josiah fifty-six
acres—Further granted to Joseph Pratt & Ebenezer Coleman
their first Division * * *—Nextly granted to Benjamin
Skinner a home lott.

At the meeting Jan. 21 : 1703 Granted to Joseph Wright
his first division of upland—Further granted to John Bacor his
first Division of upland—Nextly granted to James brown his
first Division. Nextly granted to James Taylor his Division
for one hundred pound Right on the east side of that granted
to his father Stebbins—Nextly granted to Richard Carrier his
Division of upland * * * Nextly granted to Joshua
Wheeler a home lott—Nextly granted to Moses Rowley his
Division of meadow in the meadow called Emenses meadow—
Nextly granted to Nathll Kellogg six acres—

At a Town meeting April first 1703 Granted to Thomas Day
the lott that was formerly granted to Joseph Chamberlin—

At a Town meeting Dec. 30th 1702—The Town voted that
there should be a highway on the south side of Ebenezer Dib-
bles home lott to go to the meadow—Nextly granted to John
Adams & Joseph Pumery * * * Nextly granted Andrew Carrier a home lott on the south side of the highway
against Goodman Kilborns Lott—Provided he cometh of the
Hill—further the Town grant that he shall have a two hundred
pound lotment—Nextly it was voted that the first devision of
upland next the home Lotts shall be 30 acres to the hundred
pound Lotment—

At a meeting held in Colchester May 28th 1702 it was voted that Mr. John Stebbins should have one hundred acres of land lying at the south end of the meadow called Stebbin:s meadow only there shall be a conveniant highway betwixt that and the meadow and he is to have no more land untill the rest of the Inhabitants are made equal with him—

At a Legal Town meeting held in Colchester Feb. the 3d. 1702 In consideration that Mr Nathaniel Foot is taken away by Death and thereby incapable to perform the articles of Settlement the Town have voted to take his lott into their own hands—further it was voted to grant the lott aforesaid unto Nathl Foot son of Nathl. Foot deceased—At the meeting aforesaid granted unto Shubel Rowley a parsell of land—At the meeting aforesd. granted John Hopson a home lott where he has built—

At a meeting held in Colchester August 20th 1702 Granted unto Eben. Coleman that lott which was John Gillets provided he doth forthwith make improvements & set up a Tan Yard in the Town and settle in the Town with all convenient speed—

At a Legal town meeting held in Colchester Oct. 29 : 1705. It was voted that whereas there was a Thanksgiving appointed to be held on the first thursday of november and our present circumstances being such that it cannot with conveniency be attended on that day it is therefore voted and agreed by the inhabitants as aforesaid considering the thing will not be otherwise than well resented that the second thursday of Nov. aforesaid shall be set apart for that service—At the Town meeting aforesaid it was voted and agreed by the inhabitants aforesaid that the matter of our difference with the Indians about our lands should at this present be left with the Rev. Mr John Bulkley to bring the sd difference to a composition—

At a Legal town meeting held in Colchester April 12 : 1705 granted unto Thomas Brown his first Division of upland—"

The following are specimens of the Recording of Michaell
Taintor of "Brainford," Conn., (father of Micaiell Taintor,
Esq., of Colchester) who was Recorder of Brainford for several
years previous to A. D. 1672, in which year he deceased.

"ffeb: 6th: 1667 Sargent John Ward hath Sould: and
Alenated vnto John Potter all his deuision of meddow Laying
att Scotes Cape meddow: Commonly so called: wch peece of
meddow is fower Ackeres: more or Lese: & itt is bounded by
Mathew Moulthrop on the north & by a ffence and bounded by
Danill Dod on the South: and the Saide John Potter is for to
pay Rates for this meeddow to the Towne of Brainford.

June the 10th: 1669 Mich: Taintor sould Allened & sett
ouer vnto John Potter: his haiers: Exectors Adminestrators
& Assings his Deuison of medow Laying att Scotts Cape
medow: & by some called mosceto Coue: being one Acker &
halfe more or Lese: being bounded by Samuiell Wards medow
westerly: & by: ye medow wch was Samuill Rose Easterly:
& by: vpland northerly & by: a Cricke: Easterly: also: ye
saied Mich: Taintor: hath sould vnto ye said John Potter:
ye ffence yt did belong vnto ye medow aboue.menshond—

June the 10th: 1669: John Rogers Exchanged his medow
yt he bought of Daniell Dod wch peece of medow Layes att
Scotts Cape medow: being bound by yt medow wch was·Rich-
ard Hrison easterly & by vpland northerly: & by ye farm
Riuer southerly & by John Potters medow westerly: all wch
parsells of medow the sayed John Rogers hath Allenated & sett
ouer vnto John Potter his haires execetors Adminestrators &
Assings for euer quiatly to Injoy for & in Consideration of a
peace of medow yt The saied John Potter bought of Samuill
Rose & Mich: Tayintor: ye wch medow layes att Scotts Cape
medow: & by some Called moscetto Coue being bound by vpland northerly: & by Sam Ward westerly & by a Cricke
easterly: & by a Cricke Southerly—

Know All men by these prsents yt I Daniell Rose of Weath-
ersfeild in ye County of Hartford haue sould Allinated & sett

ouer vnto Eliazar stinte of Brainford in ye County of New
Hauen: my house & Barne: Oorcheat & home Lotts wth my
Lott of medow Laying att Harrisons medow: being ffower
Ackers more or Less: & my Lott of medow Laying /att ye
Indian Necke being 3 Ackers more or Lesse: wth three Rod
of generall ffence: And ffor & in Consideration hearof ye saied
Eliazar Stinte. is for to pay or Cause for to be payed vnto the
saied Daniell Rose: his haiers Exectors Administrator or Assings The full & Just som of fforty & two Pounds ye wch is
for to be paied in manor as ffolloweth: yt is to say one fowereth
part in good wintor wheat att ffower shillinges & sixe penc pr
bushell: & one fowerth part in good peass att three shillings
& six penc pr bushell: & one fowerth part in good And Mar-
chantabell poork: att three Pounds & ten shillings pr barrell:
and one fowerth part in neat Cattell: att Corne prise: the
Cattell are ffor to be vnder ten yeare old: & in case yt thay
can not Agree betwene themselues: the Cattell are for to be
prised by two men): Twenty and one pounds of the Afore
saied fforety and two pounds is for to be payed here in Brainford: vnto the saied Daniell Rose: or his assinges: in some
house where the saied Daniell Rose shall Appoynte: the wch
is ffor to be paied: one the fiue & Twenteth day of March
next Insueing the date hereof: wch will be in ye yeare 1671:
And the other Twenty & one pounds is for to be paied vnto ye
saied Daniell Rose or his Assinges here in Brainford on the
twenty & fifth day of March in ye yeare 1672: att some house
where the saied Daniell Rose Shall Appoynt, All wch housing
& barne: & Oorcheat & home Lotts And medowes aboue men-
shoned: I do accknowledge ffor to haue sould & Allinated &
set ouer ynto the saied Eliazar Stinte: his haires Exectors
Adminestrators & Assings: for his owne proper Right—ffreely
& quiatly & peaceabely for to Injoy the same for euer, And
wthout molistation to haue & to hould itt: for his owne for
euer,: in Wittnesse hereof the saied Daniell Rose hath here-
vnto sett his hand & seeall this 25: day of March: one Thou-

&and sixe hundred & seuenty—Daniell Rose. Signed Seealled:
and deliuered in ye prsents of vs: Mich: Taintor Thomas
Harrison "

" Brainford ye 9th day of ffebr 1670—This Towne hath
ffreely Giuen & Granted vnto William Rosewell of New-Ha-
uen Marcht (merchant.—c. m. t.) & to his heires for euer Oone
Parcell or neck of vpland: bounded one ye Northeast by a
deepe fall in ye Rockey hummocke: on ye northwest sid of ye
Beuer swompe: ffrom thence alongst a swampe or Gully yt
Leads into a deepe Coue of ye ffurnace Pond on ye Westerne
sid: bounded by the sd ffurnace Pond: and one ye southerne
side by yt wch was formerly called ye Beauer brooke & one ye
Easterne side by Beauer Swamp, also one Necke or poynte of
vpland on ye southerly side of ye Beauer brooke wch is bounded
by two great trees one of yem a wallnute tree: the other A
stooping white oak wch are to be marked out: & by a straight
Line runing frrom ye Beauer brooke through these two trees
vntell itt falls in with the beauer swampe: ffurther ye Towne
doth grant vnto ye saied Roswell & his heires for euer One full
fowerth Pte (part.—c. m. t.) of the beauer swampe wch shall
be drowned to ye killing of ye (trees?)—And vnderwood that
growes thereon by meanes of a damen: made at ye charge of
ye saied Roswell or his order: And the Towne is further to
maintayne & vphold ye Labours and Servants of ye sd Roswell:
with all ye Power they haue in ye quiet & peacable Carrying
on of the damme and otherwise Relateing to ye sd swampe and
vpland, The saied Rosewell is to haue his Oone fowerth Pte of
ye saied beauer swamp Joyning to his neck of vpland from the
beauer damme to his Northeaster moste bounds of ye sd neck of
vpland or otherwise as hee & they Towne shall Agree: And
the towne doth further engage to bare theyr three fowerth Pte
of ye Charge of ye Divideing the swamp & to Lay out the saied
Roswells one fowerth Pte vnto him when hee or his heires shall
desier itt to be done: & yt hee shall haue Liberty of high

13*

wayes & Commonage for his Cattell & stooke (stock.—C. M. T.)
& A drift waye to ye Northeast wards : doeing no damage to
Ptiucler men : ffor And in Consideration whereof ye s iied
William Roswell his Labouers seruants or Assings is to m ke
a sufficent Damme & sluce for ye Drowning & drayning of as
much of the saied swampe as hee can so as ye waste watter
may Run out of The nicke in ye Lowest place digging a small
Channell if need Requier : And to maientayne ye sd damme
for ye terme of seven years from ye tim of ye ffinishing thereof :
And to begin ye worke this ensueing Summer & to finish ye
damme wthin three yeares from the day of ye date hereof Ac-
counted : or elce the Land to Returne to ye use of ye Town
againe. Recorded by order "—

The conditions of the foregoing Grant (viz. the making "of
a sufficient Damme & sluce ") were fulfilled by Wm. Rosewell
as appears by a subsequent writing, in the hand of Eleazar
Stent, to wit,—

" At a generall " meeting of the Inhabetants of the Towne of
Branford 29 April one thousand six hundred seventy and Three
at the Request of Mr William Rosewell of Newhaven Mar-
chant : The Inhabitants of the said Towne did then & there
appoint the Select men of the Towne to take Cogniscence of the
Damm & sluce made by the said Roswell (or at his Cost &
Charges) for the drowning & draining of the Beaver swomp
as may more at large appeare by a Record of agreement made
between the said Towne and the said william Rosewell bearing
date the Ninth day of february In the year of our lord 1670 in
persuance whereof we the select men of the said Towne of
Branford appearing at the said Damm and sluce of the Beaver
swomp made at the charge of the said Roswell this fifth day of
may In the year of our lord one thousand six hundred seventy
and three do find the said Damm and sluce finished according
to his agreement made with the Towne witness our hands William Hoadllie The marke S of Samuell Ward "

Our ancestors spelt the same name variously as the following writing shews—

"July 12—1667 Laurance Ward sould his house and land both vpland and medowes fences wayes waters and water Coureses even his whole accomedations that hee hath in brandfoord to Mr. John Collins of riuers mouth witnes my hand Laurance Ward—august the 10. 67 hee was voted in a towne meeting to be accepted to be a planter in the towne"

The celebrated "New Plantation & Church Covenant" of Brainford, was written by Michaell Taintor, and a portion of the signatures are in his hand. A transcript of it is as follows, viz:

"Jana.y 20th 1667 Forasmuch as yt it Appeares yt the vndertaking & the settlement of this place of Brainford was Secured by & for men of Congregationall principles as to Church order according to ye platforme of disceplaine agreed on by the Senate in 48: or thare aboutes drane from ye word of god in ye which wee yt yett Remaine hear can say wee have found much peace And quiatnes to or (our) great Comfort for ye wch wee desier for to bless god & yt itt may so Remaine vnto such as do Continue thaire abode in this place & to Such as Shall Come in to fill vp ye Roumes of those yt are Remoued & yt do intend for to Remoue from this place of Brainford. We all do see Cause now ffor to agree yt an orthodexe minester of yt Judgment shall be called in and settled Amongste vs— The gathering of Such A Church shall be Incouraged—The vpholdment of Such Church Officeors shall not want pporshanall supplye & maintainence According to Rull—We will not in Any wise Incroch vpon or disturbe their Liberties in so walking from time to time & att all times—Nor will wee bee any wayes Iniurious vnto them in ciuill or Ecclesticall Respectes & this wee ffreely andwolentarily Ingage our selues vnto Jointly & seurally so Long as wee Remayne Inhabitantes in this place & thus wee bind our Selues vnto by our Subscription vnto this Agreement—It is also Agreed yt whosoever shall Come for purchise or Admitted a ffree planter hear shall so Subscribe befor his Admittance or his Bargine Vallid in Law Amongst vs—Jasper Crane John Wilford Tho. Blachly Samuill Plum Mich : Taintor John Collens Mich : Pamer John Ward John Linsley John Robins Jonathan Rose George Adames John Whithead Samuill Ward Edward ffrisbee Henry Gratwick Mathew Bickatt Thomas Harison Thomas Whedon Georg Seward (So far " Mich : Taintor " wrote the signatures to the foregoing instrument, drawn up by himself, and of which he was doubtless the author.—c. m. t.) Robart Foot George Page Thomas Gutsell Daniell Swaine Samuell Pond Isaac Broadley Edward Ball William Hoadle Eleazar Stent John Rogers Samuell Bradfeld John Charles Sigismond Richals William Rosewell Edward Barker Peter Tyler Anthony Howd John Adames Thomas Sargent Moses Blachly Jan Worters John ffrisbe John Linsley Junr William Maltbie John Rose Bartholomew Goodrich John Taintor Francis Tyler."—

APPENDIX.

"A List of the Polls &c for the 1st Society" (Colchester) "for 1787. Jonathan Bigelow Nehemiah Gillet Ebnr Kellogg Junr Nathan Williams James Bigelow Richard Skinner Jr David Burnham Russel Gillet Joseph Gillet Junr Daniel Bulkley Stephen Brown Nathl Clark Gideon Lomis Gersham Bulkley David Bulkley Hannah Fuller Asa Swan Roger Bulkley Joseph Gillet Chauncey Wells John Bulkley Ebenr Kellogg Isham Chapman Elipht Davenport Charles Taintor Elijah Fuller Joshua Bulkley Ela Gillet Gersham Bulkley Junr Abner Chapman Asa Baker Darius Clark Jonathan Sabins Jonathan Deming Saml Hassard Amasa Kellogg John Watrous Thomas Skinner Joseph Foot Amos Kellogg John Pratt Daniel Pratt Joseph Taylor Elisha Kellogg Allen Wightman John & Wm Bulkley Zebulon Strong Rozel Chamberlin John Kellogg Theodore Waters Joseph Isham Jr Elihu Clark Thomas Vibber Lemuel F. Vibber Noah Colman Charles Bulkley 2d. Daniel Watrous Charles Taintor Jr. Dudley Wright Wm Townsend John Breed Sam. Bridges Abigail Worthington John R. Watrous Nehemiah Daniels Ezek.l Daniels Mary Kellogg Dan.l & Steph.n Foot Noah Pomroy Darius Hills Joseph Hills Hosea Foot Reuben West Mary Marriner Thos. F. Crouch John Taintor Thankful Thompson Wm Hall Daniel Kellogg Eleazer Edes John T. Otis Nath.l Otis John Button Ezra Clark Obed Alvord Elijah Northam Elisabeth Kilborn Edmond Bridges David Kilborn B. & J. N. Beadle Abner Kellogg Jeremiah Mason James F. Mason Abner Hills Deliverance Waters John Otis Joseph Bulkley Asa Archer Elizabeth Foot Justin Little John Wells Jr Uzziel Foot Jeremiah Foot Daniel Isham Benj.n Hatch Jonathan Keeny Solomon Wolcott John Chamberlin John Cavarly Joshua Hall Amos Randall Daniel Judd David Wyles Benj.n Quiterfield Charles Bulkley Israel Newton Junr. Eliph.t

Bulkley Ezra Clark Junr Israel Newton 3d. Ephraim Clark
Habakuk Foot Dudley Wright Jr. John Clark Timo. Judd Pier-
pont Bacon Elihu Warner Sam. Church 2d Oliver Warner Asa
Treadway Ephraim Wells Daniel Bulkley Junr Job Taber
W.d Sarah Wells George Palmer Joab Beebe Elias Palmer
Jr. Phlilip Cavarly Josh.a Morgan Jona. Morgan 2d. John
Newton Jr John Palmer Israel Newton Amos Wells Asa New-
ton Elijah Worthington Jr. Joel Bigelow Elijah Worthington
Dan Worthington Samuel Lomis Benj.n, Wm & Christo.
Eliery Gilbert Denison Christo. Dean Joseph Webb Israel
Lomis W.m Bulkley Peleg Ransom Wid. Ann Wells Martin
Wells Solomon Scovil Elisha Scovil David Scovil Elias
Palmer John Treadway Ama Ransom Wid. Daniel Welch Jr.
Elijah Kilborn Elisha Bigelow Asahel Newton John Cavarly
Jr. Wm Worthington Samuel Church Nathan Warner Stephen
Rossetter Asa Bigelow Elisha Dodge Oliver Brown Peter
Graves Jr. Wm Thompson George Dodge Jesse Craw Samuel
Church Jr. Anna Church Israel W. Wells John Wright Robert
Bramble Eliph t Gillet Daniel Colman Russell Kellogg Nath.l
Chamberlin Jr. Joseph Wright Jonathan Watrous Asa Graves
Daniel Clark Daniel Pratt Jr. Nath Chamberlin Isaiah Munn
Samuel Kellogg Joseph Johnson Charles Foot Daniel Bennet
Benj.n Munn Miles Wright Azariah Wright Ephraim
Little Ambrose Strong John 'Elliot Esq.r Shubael Clark
Daniel Whitney Richard H. Huntley."
' "List of the Polls &c for the Parish of Westchester for the year
1787. Noah Skinner Ezra Bigelow Caleb Gifford Joseph Day
Jr. Judah Scovil Sam.l Carrier Joseph Crocker Dan.l William
Sam.l Isham Daniel Pratt 3d. Joseph Day Weeks Williams
John Carrier Samuel Brown Adonijah Foot Elijah Williams
Timothy Waters Benj.n Adams Jr. Israel Kellogg John Isham
Asa Day Amasa Mitchel Samuel Skinner Aaron Barbur Elea-
zer & Eleazer Dunham Jr. Adriel Sabins, Eldad Sabins Jon.a
Bass Abraham Day Henry Waters Elijah Day Benj.n Hun-
tington Noah Isham Stephen Skinner Noah Skinner Jr. Knight
Sexton John Ackley George Sexton Robert Young Eph.m
Scovel Reuben Scovel Darcas Niles Nath.l Warner Jr. Joseph
Carrier Jona. Northam Jr. Robert Shattuck Susannah Gates
Sarah Yeamans Elijah Smith Joseph Whitmore Joseph Fuller
Simon Brainerd Jr. Ezra Ramsdale Stephen & William Brain-
ard Isaac Isham Isaac Isham Jr. Green Bigsby Sally Yeamans
Thomas Shaw Simeon & Timo. Crocker David Yeamans

Amasa Day Ezekiel Lord Charles Williams John Williams
Phineas Sabins Judah Lewis James Sexton Reuben Foot Uriah
Carrier Henry Champion Esq. Henry Champion Jr. Jehiel
Isham Nath.l Foot Jr. David Shattuck Stephen Brainard Jr.
Nath'l & Aaron Foot Erastus Worthington Samuel Loomis
Jonathan Dunham Joseph Isham John Bigelow John Bigelow
Jr. Joseph Loomis John Mitchel Solomon Loomis John Elliot
Esq.r John Blish Tho.s Williams John Isham Jr. Joseph Ran-
som John Olmsted Gad Worthington Amasa Brown Cephas
Cone John Day Josiah Cridenton Ambrose Niles Israel Skin-
ner James Mc. Cracken Jacob Babbit John Staples Benjamin
Staples Isaac Jones John Skinner Josiah Foot Elijah Staples
Jr. David Adams—"

" List of the Polls &c for the Parish of New Salem for the
year 1787. Elias Worthington Asa Worthington Israel Bulk-
ley Nath.l Otis (Mont) Joshua Rathbun Nath.l Harris David
Ferman Freedom Chamberlin John Ferman Daniel Gates
Ebenezer Lathrop Oliver Wells John Way Peter Bulkley
Langford Cartey Samuel Gates W.d Catharine Holms Samuel
Way John Cartey Jr. Ebenezer Rogers Abraham Randall Levi
Way James Williams Jeremiah Marshall Daniel Gardner
William Wells Joshua Way John Marshall Benja.n Randall
Clark Cartey Joseph Harris Rufus Randall Jr. Asahel Newton
Jr. Abner Chapman Jr. Abel Rathbun Silvester Randall
Rufus Randall Peter Bulkley Jr. Silas Stark Uriah Lathrop
(Boz.) Asa Randall Joseph Black Robert Douglass Robert
Henry John Holms Sam.l Rathbun John Douglass Thomas
Gates John Tennant John Deathick Abraham Avery Marvin
Gates Joshua Rathbun Jr. W.d Abigail Treadway Jonathan
Rathbun John Henry George Holms Nathan Stark Daniel
Fitch Elias Randall Moses Rathbun Samuel Holms Thomas
Fitch Elijah Kilborn Bond Bigelow Jacob Buell Ezra Brown
Wm Chapman Jonathan Dodge Jr—Gustin Walter Gustin James
Hamilton Gurdon Hamilton Amos Jones Jabez Jones Jabez
Jones Jr. John Loomis John Newton Elias Peck David Purple
Bliss Ransom Asabel Ransom James Ransom Zebulon Water-
man Daniel Dodge John Cartey Elisha Chapman John Fox
Benj.n Morgan Ichabod Chapman Jona. Chapman Ichabod
Chapman Jr. Caleb Clark Asa Daniels Elihu Dodge Wm
Gardner James Hambleton Abiel Hambleton Eli Harris Amos
Jones Jr. Hez.k Kilborn Amasa Kilborn Daniel Lothrop Joseph
Lathrop Edward Loveridge David Loveridge Abner Lov-

eridge Wm Loveridge John Loveridge Noah Loveridge
Sam.l Morgan Wm Morgan W.d Abigail Morgan Thomas
Miller Thos. Miller Jr. Wm Miller Andrew Oliver Wd
Sarah Peck Amasa Ransom Wm Ransom Israel Ransom
Irenius Ransom Job Rathbun Thos. Shaw David Treadway
Elijah Treadway Isaiah Treadway James Treadway Alpheas
Treadway John Williams Jr. Joel Worthington Samuel Rogers
Elias Harris Wm Welch Gideon Chapman Thomas Brown
Daniel Shaw Freeman Gates John Scott—"
"List for Marlborough Society for 1787. Samuel Adams
David Bigelow Elijah Buell Jr. Elisha Buell Joseph Berry
Daniel Bigelow Azariah Bigelow Zelotis Bigelow Wd. Esther
Blish Ezra Blish Asa Blish Joshua Bolles Thos. Carrier Senr.
Thos. Carrier Junr. Benj.n Curtice Benj.n Curtice Jr. Isaac
Carrier Ezra Carter Eleazar Carter Joseph Carrier Jr. James
Caton Henry Dayton Amos Dean Jr. Timothy Dutton Marvin
Dayton Abner Dean Jesse Eames Wd. Patience Eells John
Eells Saml. Finley Comfort Goff 2d. Charles Goff Comfort
Goff Saml. D. Goff Squire Goff Enos Horsford Lebbeus
Hills Jr. Daniel Horsford Thomas Hills Jacob Ingraham Levi
Dunham Daniel Judd Jr. David Kneeland Moses Kellogg
Epaphras Lord Epaphras Lord Jr. Theodore Lord John B.
Lord Ichabod Lord Elisha Lord, David Miller Ebenr. Macall
Daniel Macall Jacob Macall Solomon Phelps Jr. Ashbel
Phelps Benjn. Root Eben Strong David Strong David Skinner
Wm Stoddard John Tennant Jr. John Taintor Jr, Wd. Lois
Tracy Lazarus Waters Weeks Williams Asa Foot Esqr. Jona.
Ingraham Samuel Cone Hepzibah Foot Joel Phelps Amos
Burrows Timothy Phelps Wm Buell Elijah Buell."

We have ascertained where some more of the early settlers
were from, viz.: Thomas Beebe, of New London; Nathaniel "Cahone," (Calhoun,) from Warwick, R. I; Philip
Caverlee, of Lebanon: John Chapman, from New London: James Crocker, from Barnstable; Joseph "Dalee," from
"Prouedenc"; Thomas Day, from Hartford; Benjamin Fox,
from New London; Daniel Galusiah, from Weston; Joseph
Harrington, of Watertown; James Harris, from New Loudon
(1717); John Hopson, from Rhode Island; Isaac Jones, from
Weston; Samuel Knight, from Plainfield; Benjamin Lewes
(Lewis), from Falmouth; Robert Menter, from Lyme; Mor-
gans, from New London; James Mun, from Springfield; Robert Stapels, from Lyme; William Worthington, from Hartford.

www.ingramcontent.com/pod-product-compliance
Lightning Source LLC
Chambersburg PA
CBHW020558270326
41927CB00006B/894